Also by Leslie Linsley

Custom-Made

Fabulous Furniture Decorations

Wildcrafts

The Decoupage Workshop

Scrimshaw

Decoupage: A New Look at an Old Craft

Decoupage for Young Crafters

Decoupage On . . .

Army/Navy Surplus: A Unique Source of Decorating Ideas

Photocraft

New Ideas for Old Furniture

THE GREAT BAZAAR

Leslie Linsley

Photos by Jon Aron

Delacorte Press/New York

Acknowledgment

In the preparation of this book I received much help
from many people who have been involved with the
world of bazaars and crafting. All the wonderful suggestions, friendly letters, contributions of work, and expert
advice have made it possible to present a more com-
prehensive book. I am especially grateful to my mother,
Ruth Linsley, who helped make up so many of the
projects.

Published by Delacorte Press
1 Dag Hammarskjold Plaza
New York, N.Y. 10017

The projects on the following pages courtesy of The
Consumer Products Division, Borden Chemical: 96, 98,
151, 162, 164, and 166. Photograph on page 138 courtesy of *Family Circle*.

Manufactured in the United States of America

First printing

Book design by Jon Aron

Library of Congress Cataloging in Publication Data

Linsley, Leslie.
  The great bazaar.

  Includes index.
  1. Handicraft. 2. Bazaars, Charitable.
I. Title.
TT157.L4844   745.5′068′8   80-39802
ISBN: 0-440-03077-3

Contents

Contents

Planning a Bazaar

A successful bazaar doesn't happen by accident. According to the National Endowment for the Arts, private individuals in this country supply 80 percent of the support for nonprofit cultural organizations by giving their time, talents, and money. People who plan fund-raising events are an imaginative group. They find an infinite number of ways to stage these activities from auctions, craft fairs, and flea markets to elaborate formal balls and decorator showcase houses. Millions of dollars are raised by private citizens, who are as personally concerned over every penny raised as if the money were going into their own bank accounts.

All kinds of groups put on fund-raising events: service clubs, churches, schools, charities, local organizations, political groups, and individuals with personal interests in common. The spring is a popular time for craft fairs because the craftworkers can take advantage of good weather to display their work outdoors. It is a way to show and sell what they have spent the winter producing.

Christmas bazaars take place at almost every church or school in the country and are anticipated by everyone in the community. Most of us have learned from experience which bazaars are the best and save our shopping for these events.

If you are involved with planning a bazaar you will want to develop a positive reputation for your group so that the affair will be well attended. The support and enthusiasm from your community will ensure success.

The most familiar and popular bazaars are craft bazaars, which usually offer, in addition, home-baked goods, recycled toys, used books, a white elephant booth, and plants. This is the kind of bazaar that this book will concern itself with. There are professional fund raisers who raise money for large projects, but we're addressing ourselves to the more usual, homegrown church or Scout bazaar.

State Your Goals

While everyone wants to make money during a bazaar, the most important thing is to have a good time. The environment that is created for an affair like this begins long before opening day. If there's been disagreement, haphazard planning, mismanagement, or lack of enthusiasm, it will culminate in a mediocre bazaar. What you want to achieve from the first planning meeting is a feeling of unity and goodwill. This might seem obvious, but a few tips may help. For example, when deciding who will take charge of what, everyone should do what he or she enjoys and feels capable of doing. In this way the jobs will be efficiently carried out.

Not long ago I was in charge of organizing a craft show in a cooperative gallery. I was familiar with the exhibitors' work but didn't know the artists personally. It was decided that during the week-long event various craftworkers would demonstrate their work. I made a list of several different crafts that would be of interest to the visiting public and contacted the craftworkers to set up demonstration times for each.

I assumed that everyone would welcome the opportunity to show off his or her technique and didn't think to ask if this would be a problem. After the show was over, one woman confided that it had been a horrible experience for her. She was not used to explaining her craft, did not enjoy answering questions when put on the spot, and, worst of all, was so shy that just sitting there made her extremely uncomfortable. "Why didn't you say something when I first called you?" I asked. She explained that she had been too shy to do even this and felt obligated to participate when asked. She would have been better off doing some setting-up work behind the scenes.

If raising money is a major goal, you should try to set an amount to strive for. In this way you can figure out how much you might realize from the sales and how much you will have to solicit in donations. A certain attendance figure might be another goal. From here you can plan publicity posters, announcements, etc., accordingly. Well-defined objectives will help you realize your goals.

Organizing

Jeanne O'Neill is an experienced church bazaar organizer. She has helped to raise thousands of dollars for worthy causes over the past twenty years and says that the bazaars she has cochaired have been the most unforgettable experiences she's had. "The best advice I can offer for a good bazaar is to be well organized," she says. "There are certain basic booths that are always popular. You should include the latest craft craze as this changes from year to year and within different areas of the country. Most booths require workshops that are set up well ahead of time. And by the way, this is probably the most fun. Get-togethers or fun shops, as we used to call them, are great for making new friendships."

To get the ball rolling, form an initial committee of a few interested people who will then solicit others to work in the various areas needed. Write a newsletter that is chatty and enthusiastic, telling all the specifics you can at that point. This will be an informal introduction to the affair and should be sent several months ahead, for instance, during the summer for a Christmas bazaar. Since the initial group will be writing the letter, this is a good opportunity for organizing your thoughts. When you have to explain to others, in writing, what the bazaar is all about, it helps you organize and determine exactly what it will be.

Map out the general areas of interest, and decide what jobs will need volunteers. In your letter suggest that each person be thinking about what he or she would like to do for the bazaar. Don't overlook the children. There are many projects that can be designated for different age-groups. Let the people know that a committee member will call on the phone within two weeks of their receiving the letter. A sample letter will follow this section. Use it as a guide for composing your letter, substituting the specifics of your bazaar.

During your first meeting of the core group allow everyone to choose what tasks fit his or her talents or interests best. Elect one person who is efficient, personable, and reliable to oversee the whole bazaar. Or you may decide to have two people share the chair. This person or persons should not be expected to be concerned with details. There should be a specific person heading each group who can be called on to get specific jobs done. Committees could include the following:

1. Decoration (signs, posters, table coverings)
2. Booth construction, if needed

3. Publicity
4. Finances
5. Garbage cleanup
6. Refreshments
7. Individual booths (how many, what kinds, how they should be located in relation to one another)

Essentials for Success

The following suggestions were offered by many people who have been involved with bazaars, fairs, Scout troop events, and flea markets. When an event has not been successful, there was usually a problem in one of these areas:

1. Everyone should feel personally involved.
2. When asking for work to be done, be specific about the job. State when it must be done.
3. Decide on quality standards, if possible, and try to maintain them throughout.
4. Leave plenty of time for planning.

If, for example, a fair is not adequately publicized, attendance will be low. This creates a dull atmosphere, few sales, and lack of enthusiasm on the part of the exhibitors. If no one is in charge of the overall appearance, a bazaar can end up looking like a giant rummage sale when the intention was to create a gift-buying environment.

At the Winter Olympics in Lake Placid terrible problems were created by inadequate planning for parking space. Check with the local police to see if you will need any special permits, and arrange for plenty of garbage disposal areas. In our enthusiasm to create exciting booths it's easy to overlook these things.

A Checklist for Planning

The following is a checklist to refer to. Use it as a guide, and add anything to it that will be useful for your specific problems.

1. Set a date. If outdoors, have a rain date.
2. Pick a location.
3. Select a person or persons to be in charge.
4. Determine committees.
5. Plan a theme, if desired.
6. Organize workers and plan booths.
7. Consider rentals.
8. Write press releases; plan to take photos to go with the publicity stories.
9. Plan and print posters, announcements, labels, bags, etc., if needed.
10. Establish an accounting system.
11. Decide how the money will be handled. Will each booth be responsible, or will there be a central "pay" booth?
12. Think about booth placement for convenient traffic flow.
13. Is someone needed to direct the parking of cars?
14. Get as many local businesses involved as possible. This could mean donation of goods and services, posters in store windows, financial assistance.

**This Way!
to the Fair on Fair Street**
August 14th

Teaser ads for St. Paul's Church Fair

"WOULD YOU BUY A USED BOOK FROM THIS MAN?"

**You certainly CAN on August 14th
at the ST. PAUL'S CHURCH FAIR!**

(and we could still use anything used
so just call this man at 257-6608,
as soon as you can.........thank you.)

Photographs by Beverly Hall

"Teaser" ads are placed in local papers well in advance of the event. Notice that contributions of books are solicited while also advertising the fair.

11

Get Ready for Christmas in July

Relaxed? Feeling lazy? Summer is really here. The ironing mounts up; the house stays a little messier with the kids home. We snatch at shortcuts for easy, cool meals.

And who gives a thought to Christmas ornaments or making winter caps and mittens when the only comfortable attire is a bathing suit? Yes, summer is meant for lazy living. We agree. BUT . . . it's a different story when it comes to St. Norbert's Christmas Bazaar.

On that score we are hoping you will be full of boundless enthusiasm in donating your time and talents to make this year's bazaar a scintillating success. We need your homemade goodies and your handcraft work. The sole purpose of the bazaar, sponsored by the Women's Club, is to raise funds for the parish. We also expect to have a real good time.

During the next two weeks you will be called on to sign up for the following booth of your choice. Some require working through the summer at weekly fun shops; others will need your services at bazaar time. Checking your choices ahead of time (perhaps over coffee this morning) will save our callers considerable time.

Won't all of you please emerge from your hot-weather lethargy and help us make a successful bazaar? You'll find fun, new friends, and a sense of accomplishment by being a willing worker. Anyone with special talents or a suggestion that has proved to be a success, please let your caller know. This is everyone's bazaar and we want you to be part of the activities. If you work and are on a tight schedule, we have a list of things that can be done quickly, in snatches of spare time, but are no less important. Let us hear from you. If you can't be involved in the planning, give an hour or two of relief to a booth sitter on bazaar day.

Bakery Booth

Homemade pies, cakes, relishes, cookies, and bread. There is such a demand for homemade bread! If you can bake bread, please make special mention of it when called.

Candies

Popcorn balls (over 300 were sold before noon last year). Taffy apples can be purchased cheaper than they can be made, so we need cash donations to get them. Fudge is always popular. Anyone willing to make candy in quantity is asked to make special mention of it when called.

Christmas Decorations

Wreaths	Festive candles
Centerpieces	Religious figures
Door decorations	Angels
Unusual tree ornaments	Santa figures

We need volunteers for the fun shops.

Please take the time.

Plant Booth

Any size or shape flower containers

Live plants

Plant arrangements (live or dry)

Potting materials

Does anyone make hanging planters, clay pots, baskets?

Grab Bag

We are striving to repeat last year's success in this booth. We are asking for toys valued under $1 for ages one to twelve. These items need not be gift wrapped, but we need at least one item from each family to ensure the success of this booth. If you prefer to make a cash donation, the committee will make the purchases for you. Let us give every child the opportunity to make a purchase from this MERRY booth.

Stitchery Booth

If you can sew on a button, then the STITCHERY BOOTH is the place to show your talents. You may want to branch out and make some simple items that can be reasonably priced. Any ideas for pets? Knitters, we need mittens, scarves, caps, slipper socks, baby booties.

Let's form a group that meets regularly for these projects.

Handyperson's Corner

Everyone who can hold a hammer is needed to make this booth a success. Here is a list of items you may choose to make.

Birdhouses	Bookshelves	Step stools
Shoeshine kits	Name plaques	Flower boxes
Bookends	Dollhouses	Key holders

Refreshments

Coffee   Tea   Cakes   Pies   Hot Dogs   Sandwiches

Cash donations are needed for meat, rolls, bread, etc.

Baby-sitting

We need teen volunteers. Give one hour for a good cause. Pick your time. Be part of the bazaar.

Signed: Chairperson

Phone number

Publicity

In order to have a successful bazaar, people must attend. As one craftsperson I interviewed told me, "When you work hard on your projects, set up your things, and then sit all day without customers you feel terrible. I show at a lot of fairs and just assume that whoever's in charge will do whatever's necessary to bring in the people. When it doesn't happen, you're very discouraged."

Get as much publicity as possible for your event. Design and print posters well in advance of the date. Place them in store windows and in well-traveled areas of town.

If one person writes clearly, he or she should be in charge of the press release. Some knowledge of the media is helpful. Place a story about your bazaar in the local newspaper as well as in the papers in surrounding towns. Also list the facts in "Coming Events," if your paper has such a section. Large companies often print an in-house newsletter. Ask any companies in your area to include your announcement. Don't forget radio and television, if appropriate.

Preparing a Press Release

Give the most important information first. If the newspaper must cut space, you'll be sure to have the facts listed. These would include what, when, where, and why.

Make your bazaar sound as exciting as possible so that it will appeal to all ages. Talk about an interesting booth. If you have a well-known craftsperson exhibiting, do a profile on his or her work. Be specific without overloading the story. Avoid long lists of items. Tell the purpose of the bazaar, but don't go into a lengthy description unless it is the main point of interest. Talk about the most popular or unusual items. Use your imagination when describing the projects.

If you submit a photograph with the release, make it an attention getter. It might feature an event or craftworkers at a get-together. An 8 x 10 black-and-white glossy print is what most publications like to work with.

If you send the press release four weeks in advance, try to get another story in the papers the week before or a few days before the bazaar. This will be more of a "we're all ready to go" story, reminding everyone that the date is coming up. A photo could show the decorated booths in preparation for the big day.

Beverly Hall

Come to the Christmas Bazaar

Date: Time: Place:

Have you made out your Christmas shopping list yet? There are only thirty more shopping days left until Christmas! But the biggest and best shopping day promises to be Saturday, November ———. By eight o'clock that evening we'll have a gift for everyone on our list. We'll have shopped the easy and fun way by attending St. Norbert's Christmas Bazaar, the biggest and best annual event sponsored by the Women's Club.

We plan to make a day of it, using all the services provided, with, of course, a stop for a bite to eat at the Café Noel. Cochairpersons Jim White and Betty Brown are prepared for hungry shoppers all day long. There'll be coffee, hot chocolate, doughnuts at any time, with hamburgers, french fries, coleslaw for lunch and a special ham plate for dinner, for a mere $2.50.

The Christmas carols over the loudspeaker and the atmospheric decorations will put us in the holiday spirit from the very beginning. Cochairpersons Sally O'Day and Chris Conner will turn St. Norbert's School into an old-fashioned street scene, with each classroom booth showcasing its wares amid the nostalgic aura of gaslights and gabled roofs.

Anxious to start on your shopping list? Why not take a peek at ours and see how we'll shop at the different booths?

Janey: Our favorite college student will go back to school with something homemade from the GINGERBREAD HOUSE. Cochairpersons Barbara Zimmerman and Milly Ripply promise us all kinds of homemade yummy goodies.

Uncle Jim: A doll of an uncle . . . and what a plant lover! He'll be pleased with a gift from the PINE PLANTER. We can choose from an assortment of green plants, dried flower arrangements, and artificial roses. Cochairpersons Sal Hayes and Jeanne Kirk have thoughtfully provided centerpieces for the upcoming holidays.

Aunt Kay: Here's the aunt who has everything but is mad for original and "different" gifts. The GLITTER BOX solves all problems with its lovely variety of Christmas ornaments, table and door decorations, mobiles, candles—even holiday corsages. Cochairpersons Gerry Zeli and Rosemary Allister are enthusiastic over the items in their booth.

Mom and

Dad: At the BATH BOUTIQUE there'll be a wonderful assortment of monogrammed towels. Chairperson Ann

Smith and her daughter Muffy will have all kinds of wonders from soap holders and decorative soaps to unusual bath mitts and sachets.

Joe: A wonderful brother who hasn't been bitten by the do-it-yourself bug, but admires everyone else's efforts. THE HANDY WORKSHOP, chaired by Steve Markus, should provide a handmade gift for his house.

Us! We assume we're on someone's list. We know every booth will have innumerable things we'd dearly adore. THE KRIS KRINGLE KOTTAGE will be the perfect spot for our children to find gifts for us and every member of the family. Cochairpersons Bernice Johnson and Janie Carty have geared the price range of their variety of handmade articles to the buying power of children.

Now isn't that easy? And won't it be fun? We're sure you can take care of your shopping list with as much enjoyment as we will have. Join us at THE CHRISTMAS BAZAAR, Saturday, November ——, from ten in the morning to eight in the evening. See you then.

Christmas Bazaar Cochairpersons

Gerry Garmoe

Jeanne O'Neill

The best way to tap talent for a bazaar is to organize regularly scheduled workshops. In this way even the busiest people can plan to do some creative work in the time specifically set aside for it. Anyone who has been involved with a bazaar says that working together creates close friendships and is a lot of fun.

Craft socials provide an efficient way to make certain projects that are inefficient for one person to make. Some projects lend themselves to assembly-line production better than others. These are projects that usually involve several steps or a lot of preparation or a pattern that can be repeated over and over. Sometimes it means that producing this item in quantity cuts down considerably on the cost.

Even when everyone is working on separate but similar projects, like embroidery, it is practical to share materials. Also, the company of others makes the time go by quickly. By working together, time-consuming projects are more easily tackled. A quilting bee, for instance, is always enjoyable. It is much more fun for people quilting to do it in a group.

Bookbinding is another project that is not difficult to do and has always been a proved best seller at bazaars. The cost of covered note pads should be kept low, and this can be done when several people work together. This craft requires precision cutting of all pieces. Once this preliminary preparation is done, enough covered pads to fill a booth can be made quickly and efficiently.

Some projects require a variety of designs. Painted baskets can provide an opportunity for free-form expression from a few talented people. Different sizes and shapes add to the overall effect.

The result is a colorful booth that fits all the requirements for successful sales.

Most sewing projects can be done as a joint effort. If one pattern is used to make aprons, velvet bags, or bow corner boxes, variety is achieved in the choice of fabrics, colors, appliqués, and finishing details.

Some crafting techniques are impractical for a bazaar unless they are used to make items in quantity. An example of this is batik. This craft requires heating a pot of dye on the stove and melting wax. It is only efficient if you make at least ten batik T-shirts at once. The dyed baby shirts and socks on pages 37 and 44 should be made in quantity for maximum cost efficiency. They can then be decorated at a workshop.

Stenciling is a technique that many people have perfected, and it can be adapted for a group, working together. For example, the boxes on page 68 can be sanded and painted at one meeting. At the next meeting, after cutting the stencils, each person can use a different stencil to create a variety of boxes. It might take one person a week to do this, while five people can complete them in two get-togethers. Decide how many boxes will make up a display, and plan the number of workshops accordingly.

Some crafts require several steps. Often there is part of a crafting technique that one person may enjoy doing while another person may like another part. Decoupage, for example, involves painting, varnishing, and sanding as well as cutting out and designing paper elements. While I am competent at cutting very intricate flowers, my mother has far more patience for the meticulous job of achieving the fine finish required. Everyone can do something to contribute to a craft process.

The decoupage trinket boxes (page 55), recipe file (page 54), and rose-covered box (page 50) require several coats of varnish. Each must dry between coats. These are good projects for workshops. It has been my experience that at a workshop everyone contributes not only time and creative talent but also timesaving tips and ways to cut cost. It is an excellent way to pool resources.

Sometimes one person is more competent to draw or plan a design. Those who feel less creative can carry out the execution of the design. The little velvet bags, for example, can be cut, sewn, and lined by those who are expert sewers. The appliqués can then be cut and applied by others.

There is usually one perfectionist in every group. If you can tap this talent for the finishing of detailed work, it will make your projects all the more professional-looking. For example, when sewing in quantity, even the most experienced person can overlook a dangling thread or a loosely sewn button or leave off ribbon or trim—details that contribute to higher sales. Don't try to do everything. Spread the work around. This creates a feeling of unity, and everyone is involved with the bazaar's success.

Competition from co-workers can be the death of a potentially happy, successful bazaar. Attitude is everything, and it's a good idea to establish this from the beginning.

At one fair I attended in Amherst, Massachusetts, all the exhibitors were unusually friendly to one another. Often one person would ask a customer if he or she had seen a similar booth in another section. I knew a few of the craftspeople and asked one why this fair seemed so congenial. "We've all met each other over the years at other fairs," she explained. "Everyone wants to sell his or her crafts, but we also want to see the next person succeed as well. It's a lot of work to put one of these together. A craft fair is part of our folk heritage, and when we do well, it's good for the whole country. Everyone has a stake in keeping the tradition alive."

Crafts That Sell

Anyone who has ever been to a bazaar knows that one or two booths are always the most popular. They attract the most attention, maintain attendance throughout the day, and usually sell the most.

Before doing this book I decided to find out which crafts always sell, and why. I sent out letters, attended fairs, and made phone calls to get the input from the "experts," those people who have had experience in organizing bazaars, exhibiting regularly at craft fairs, or selling to stores. Some of them are professional craftspeople who own craft stores; some exhibit their work in galleries, belong to co-ops, or sell designs for craft projects through mail-order catalogs and magazines. Some write articles or newsletters and are in a position to get feedback through letters or orders. I also talked to the craft editors of the major magazines as well as marketing people who are involved with this area of sales. They all agreed that there are definite reasons why some crafts are more appealing than others. Craft projects that sell at bazaars have basic requirements, unlike those that are sold through more conventional means. They must be:

1. Easily recognized
2. Easy to make
3. Inexpensive to make, therefore accessibly priced
4. Able to be adapted to make in quantity
5. Made from materials readily available
6. Well designed
7. Have proved popularity (evidenced by repeatedly appearing in the magazines and at craft bazaars)
8. Well displayed

Most exhibitors make the things they enjoy making most and are therefore good at. The craft bazaar is a place to display that work. However, if the goal is to make money, you will have to take an objective view when deciding what you will bring to the fair. To most of us, time is valuable, and we want to have some assurance that it will pay off in monetary rewards as well as in having a good time. A crocheted afghan, for example, may be something you enjoy making. An afghan would probably have to sell for a great deal of money, and it would be worth it. But the risk of finding that person who wants to make such an expensive commitment when there is so much else to buy is too great. Also, there is no time for deliberation, as in a store. Since a bazaar is held for only one or two days, most sales occur as a result of impulse buying. You would do better modifying your technique to the making of smaller items that will sell more quickly.

Senior citizens with time to spare can put their experience to good use. Sewing skills, long practiced, can be applied to new ideas for a contemporary audience. In this case it makes sense to have some teamwork. The persons with less time to spare might create the designs and do the finishing work.

While it is advisable to be cautious about large, time-consuming, and expensive pieces as salable craft fair items, you don't have to eliminate them altogether. If you have other items that will sell quickly, use your *pièce de résistance* as a display to attract customers.

Special Crafts

I have attended practically every kind of fair along the eastern seaboard and have found that what sells in the suburbs is completely different from what sells in the city. Furthermore, certain crafts sell only in specific areas because their value is not recognized elsewhere. Ethnic crafts are an example of this.

One Ukrainian street fair I went to was sponsored by a neighborhood block association and had a definite theme. Aprons, tablecloths, and blouses were decorated with folk embroidery in the familiar black and red cross-stitch. Bakery booths sold breads, powdered cakes, and pastries. The Ukrainian painted eggs, distinguishable for their intricate designs and craftsmanship, sold quickly. I was told that the high prices do not deter sales when the buyers understand and appreciate the work.

This is also the case in seashore communities where scrimshaw is sold. Examples of this craft of etching on ivory are much sought after in summer vacation spots and on both coasts. When people are knowledgeable about what they are buying, they can evaluate price, and the craftworker doesn't have to explain why his or her wares may seem high.

In the West, Indian jewelry made of silver and turquoise is the "walkaway" item. In the South seashell wind chimes are particularly popular. Hex signs are shown throughout the Pennsylvania Dutch country, woodworking abounds in New England, and leatherworking is associated with the Southwest. Silhouettes and pastel portraits are standard money-makers everywhere. (See the Source List for silhouette material. It is surprisingly easy to do.)

Craft kit and book show how to make Ukrainian Easter eggs.

Quality

Do you want to establish a level of quality for your bazaar? A craft bazaar can be an "anything goes" affair, or you can determine what kind of image you want to project. At a flea market, for example, each person sets up his or her own area and can sell almost anything. An air of excitement emanates from this kind of environment, the element of surprise. We don't know what treasures we may uncover, and everyone expects to find a bargain. In this case, the more exhibitors, the better.

However, most craft bazaars have some guidelines that have been established by a committee. If the bazaar is held indoors and space is limited, you'll have to determine how many booths you can have. Within that space try to get as much variety as possible. The more different crafts, styles, workmanship, and price ranges the better. Put a limitation on how many items each booth can display, if necessary, and decide which crafts must be eliminated. If, for example, five people want to make the same kinds of projects, suggest that they get together to make up one booth. Each can display the best of his or her craft.

One of the best small craft shows takes place each year in Westport, Connecticut, at the Unitarian Church. The space is limited, so there is a process of elimination. The craftworkers must submit their work to a committee of knowledgeable people. The crafts that are shown have proved successful, and the quality of the show is consistent throughout. Professional craft fairs that have earned a reputation for bringing in the people maintain high standards of acceptance. The annual fair at Rhinebeck, New York, regularly receives over 1,400 applications, of which 350 are accepted.

However, at the church or Scout bazaar that most of us are familiar with, the problem is usually the reverse. If you have trouble getting enough craftwork, make up announcements and posters to place in craft shops, on church bulletin boards, and in key community places. Send an announcement to the newspaper. Specify what you are seeking, what it is for, and whom to contact.

It's a good idea to have different levels of craft proficiency. The amateur hobbyist will make up the largest group, and most of the space should be devoted to their work, but if there are some professional crafters in your community, encourage them to display their work, too. There should also be room for the first timers, those people who are making things for fun in order to be part of the bazaar. Their contributions could include things made from kits, purchased items that have been decorated, or such loosely defined crafts as recipe holders, pomander balls, potpourri, clown face painting on children, iron-on transfer T-shirts, and souvenir button making. All of these are potential money-makers but do not have to be judged on the same merits as the others.

Pricing for Profit

Most bazaars are organized for the purpose of raising money for a worthy cause. Others are planned by craftspeople who want to sell their wares for individual profit. Whatever the reasons for having a bazaar, every effort should be made to reach the stated goals. Once the event is over, most of its success is measured by how much profit was made.

How to Determine Price

There is nothing more exciting than a popular booth. This is a result of an eye-catching display of items that respond to a need or to impulse gift buying. But these items must also be easily affordable. How do you decide what price to put on your projects?

I find it helpful to work backwards. Look at your project objectively, and ask what you would pay for it. Look in the stores to see what similar things cost. Keep in mind, however, that a store can charge more because the owners have built up goodwill and cater to their customers on a regular basis. The customer pays for the services of charge accounts and packaging, even if this only means a bit of tissue and a paper bag.

Most people who come to a bazaar expect a bargain. They should feel they are getting it. In addition to fair prices, this may mean more value, better design, good craftsmanship, or a unique item. Contrary to what you might think, to sell at a bazaar you must try harder. You have a short time to sell your work, and you know very little about the buying habits of the crowd. Few of us take the time to figure out what the people in our community will respond to. Generally we make what we enjoy making in the hope that it will sell.

A good price brings more sales to a desirable product. A higher price usually restricts sales. In order to determine what you should charge for your work, keep track of all out-of-pocket expenses for making one item. Obviously you will be buying at retail, so try to project how much less the item can be made for if the materials are purchased in quantity. Be sure to account for lost or wasted material if it can't be used in another project. Figure in the cost of gas, if you drive to buy the items, and postage, if you're ordering through the mail. Keep written receipts, or pay for everything with checks.

You should also keep track of your time. At first you will invest time for planning and designing the project. This shouldn't be figured into the work, as it will be absorbed when making subsequent projects. Craftwork rarely commands a price that compensates for your time. However, a record of the time spent will help establish the final selling price.

Figure out what it costs you in out-of-pocket expenses and labor (at a moderate rate) to produce one item. Base the unit price on an estimated total production. If you make four dozen items, the unit cost should be less than that for making two items because you should be able to buy materials at a better price. (See Source List for wholesale suppliers.)

Once you establish your unit cost, you can figure out what the item would sell for if you sold it to a retail store rather than at a bazaar. Do this by doubling your unit cost. This is the wholesale price. If your unit cost is $1, the wholesale price would be $2, and the store would double it again for a retail price of $4.

However, since you are selling directly to the customer you may decide that a good price is $3.00 or $2.50. If others are selling similar items, check the prices to evaluate your estimate of what your prices should be. Conversely, if other items are selling at your price, think about whether the value is comparable.

Cutting Costs

Figure out ways to cut corners without scrimping on quality. Even if your time is donated, find efficient ways to cut time as well as cost. You may not be evaluating your time on the basis of money, but it is still valuable. Don't underestimate what you can accomplish with your time, and choose wisely where you want to spend it.

Can several of your items be made at one time? This may mean that you can order materials at a discount. You may also be able to set up a mini assembly-line production to cut time. By turning this activity into a social event, the time spent reaps rewards far beyond the monetary.

Will you sell substantially more by cutting the price of your items? If you price them too low, however, you may actually decrease the value in the eye of the customer. If you don't feel that your sales will increase by cutting the price, don't. I've been to fairs where the prices were so low that it demeaned the projects. Don't underestimate the importance of accurate pricing.

Buying Materials

We tend to pick up the little inexpensive materials we need as we make a project: a box of pins, a spool of thread, tape, etc. But you can realize a tremendous savings by buying these items from one source. If you order everything that you need

at one time, you will receive a discount from most mail-order houses and small manufacturers. This takes some planning. Estimate how much of each item you'll need, and make a list. Look under "Source List of Materials" for ordering in quantity. It's a good idea to send for several catalogs to compare prices.

If you can get together with other people and all order at once, you will realize an even greater savings. If you're working in a group, take the time to figure out what you'll all need, and leave enough time for ordering materials.

Consider how your projects will be packaged, if at all. Bags, tissue paper, and labels add to the individual cost and are practical only when purchased in quantity. Try to buy one color or one size that will accommodate all the booths. You will realize a substantial savings by ordering printed labels, bags, and flyers in quantity.

Getting Your Price

How can you boost the price? Diane Babb designs original stuffed animals. Her company is called Fuzzy Friends by Diane. For over seven years she has offered her designs at craft fairs and through her mail-order catalog. She recommends using quality fabrics to increase sales. They contribute much to the finished product, and the added cost is offset by the better price you can put on the finished toy. For example, if you buy a quarter yard of $4-a-yard fabric, the cost to make one item is $1. However, a quarter yard of $6-a-yard fabric adds only 25 cents to the overall cost, and the toy might bring back an extra $1 or more.

Often a higher price can be justified by adding interesting details. A small elegant trim enhances items made from inexpensive materials and adds to the value. If a pattern is intricate, consider simplifying it without altering the effect. All the suppliers listed at the end of the book provide patterns that have proved successful for bazaar sales.

Drawing Cards

If you are selling anything, the goal is to make money, not to lose it. If nothing sells, you have lost time, money, and the enjoyment that comes from having your work accepted.

It's a good idea to have one item that really draws. Several years ago I had a craft shop where local craftworkers displayed exquisite and expensive handwork. After two weeks of much sales resistance to what we were offering, a woman walked in carrying a large bouquet of tissue-paper flowers she'd made. Each was a giant colorful flower on a long stem. She thought they should sell for $1 apiece. We filled an umbrella stand with all of them and set it in the window. It was a wonderful attraction. Nobody left without at least one flower, and usually the customer would linger and buy a more expensive item.

Later I stocked inexpensive costume jewelry, decorated combs, and other novelties that led the customers into the other products. The less expensive items created activity and made up for the lack of steady sales of the other things.

When you have an item that sells rapidly, people are drawn to your booth to get in on the excitement. If possible, try to present a variety of projects that are priced to sell quickly.

Balloons: they create a mood and promote the bazaar

27

Basic Booths

Every bazaar has certain booths that everyone looks forward to. These stock the proved successes that are fun to prepare, sell well, and turn a good profit. They are the tried-and-true, so give each plenty of attention. The following booths are basic to all bazaars.

Food

Every bazaar has a food or bakery booth, and in certain parts of the country different items sell better than others. In fact, I have found that what sells in one area may be completely unfamiliar in another.

No fair is complete in Pennsylvania without lemon sticks. In Baltimore it's peppermint sticks. In Connecticut, where I come from, we never heard of either. Apparently people really enjoy sucking on a lemon that is stuck on the end of a candy stick which somehow sweetens the sour juice before it reaches the mouth.

In New York it is sausage and shish kebab stands, and in Mystic Seaport, Connecticut, fish patties are the thing. In Nantucket and New Bedford, Massachusetts, people sell quahog chowder and Portuguese bread, and in Florida it's key lime pie.

In California sour ball necklaces and bracelets are the big sellers. The colorful wrapped candies are tied and strung together, creating their own eye-catching display.

Christmas jams, jellies, cakes, and cookies still sell everywhere, and things that are wrapped in appealing containers do best. But the all-time universal winners are brownies and chocolate chip cookies.

When planning this booth, decide what you'll do with unsold food. It can be reduced in price at the end of the day, and then anything that's left donated to an institution such as a home for seniors, a day care center, hospital, etc.

Food Containers

There are many ways to display food. Glass storage jars come in all sizes, styles, and prices. For jams and jellies, don't forget baby jars and inexpensive jelly or juice glasses.

Tie plastic-wrapped breads with full satin ribbons and plaid, checked, or polka-dot bows. Be lavish. Tuck a mint sprig or cinnamon stick into the knot. Use colorful napkins (made from scraps) to package cookies.

Line a bread basket with fabric, and tie with a bow (see page 156). Fill with homemade bread, brownies, etc. Make pretty labels for your food. Collect interesting tins, and line them with doilies, fabric, lace, tissue paper. Use brightly colored bags tied with yarn, or stencil *The Best Chocolate Chippers* on brown sandwich bags. Paper punch a hole in the top, and tie with yarn or ribbon.

Special Christmas Food Wraps

1. Make miniature loaves of orange or cranberry bread. Suggest that these can be frozen for last-minute Christmas gifts. Make your own or buy French dish towels of red or blue and white check. Use these to wrap each little loaf. Insert the recipe under a red plaid ribbon tied in a festive bow.

2. Assemble several empty baby food jars, and paint the tops with Krylon spray paint. Glue red or

Satin-covered plant holder becomes food container

white rickrack trim around the rim of each top. Fill each jar with relish, and suggest it as a stocking stuffer.

3. Coffee cans are the perfect size to hold cookies. Glue buttons all around the outside of a can. This can be used as a button holder (and other sewing aids) once the cookies are gone. Decorate another with velvet, satin, and embroidered ribbons or bright, fat yarn. Spray paint another. Create designs with Mystik tape. Use decals or stickers such as stars from the five-and-ten.

4. Paper paint buckets are sold in hardware stores for under 50 cents. Decorate with paint, decoupage, or stencil designs.

5. Cover a cigar box or similar cardboard box with pretty fabric or paper. Line with bright tissue, and fill with cookies. Type or write the recipe or name of the items on a mailing label, and attach to the center of the lid. Tie closed with a wide white satin ribbon.

6. Pack your homemade jam in a mason jar. Tie a small decorative butter knife or spoon to the lid, and give or sell with a freshly baked loaf of bread. Wrap the bread in a French country cotton print, and tie with a contrasting ribbon.

7. Cover an oval wooden mushroom basket with contrasting ribbons into which you insert small candy canes. Use this to hold jars of relish, a loaf of bread, or cookies.

8. Use pretty ceramic jars to hold cranberry relish.

9. Make plaid taffeta drawstring bags in minutes. Fill each with a jar of canned fruit (put up in the summer when fruit is in season). Tuck a sprig of holly into the drawstring ribbon.

10. Make a decorative label with your favorite recipe typed on it. Glue this to the center of a breadboard. Coat with Krylon clear spray varnish or acrylic. Let dry. Place loaf of bread, muffins, or cookies on the board. Wrap the whole thing. The board can later be hung as a kitchen decoration and as a recipe reminder.

11. Use pretty plant pots to hold baked goods or jam jars for gift giving. Decorate plain plastic pots with decals, ribbon, simple painted designs, or a patchwork of scraps.

12. Cover an oatmeal box with greeting paper, and line with tissue paper. Fill with cookies. Coat the outside with clear varnish for a sturdy, long-lasting container. Add a label, *SNAX,* using press-on letters.

13. Using a rubber stamp and red ink pad, print *FRAGILE* in an overall pattern on plain white shelf paper. Wrap a loaf of bread or cake, and tie with a one-inch white grosgrain ribbon on which you've stamped *Fragile* repeatedly.

Plants

Plan early for this booth so you can plant seeds and create starters. The containers can be simply decorated throwaways (see Berry Baskets, page 108) or combined with the work of a potter. Be sure to have a wide range of prices so children can afford to buy a plant for Mom and Dad.

If you want to coordinate this booth, solicit donations of plastic pots and paint them with one design. (See Food Containers, page 28, for one idea.)

Purchase inexpensive goblets, glasses, vases, mugs, and cups from flea markets, garage sales, thrift shops, and the five-and-ten to hold the plants. This will give you a variety of containers in different sizes.

Spray paint wax-coated meat trays in bright colors. Place potted plants on them for a colorful display. These will catch drips when plants are watered.

Rummage

Everyone wants to get something for nothing or practically nothing. This booth is the one to look for. But you will have to be very careful when soliciting goods. When something is donated, we hate to reject it, but you should have some guidelines.

All clothing should be clean. Decide what items you will not accept. Solicit the things you feel will sell well, and stress the point that each person clean, wash, or iron what he or she donates. Used toys shouldn't have missing pieces, and it helps to tape the boxes of games closed to keep pieces intact.

Books are welcome but should be priced low. Usually 10 and 25 cents for paperbacks and 50 cents to $1 for hardcovers are about right.

All collectibles, antiques, and "junktiques" can be included here. It's a chance for everyone to do some housecleaning. Price these items to sell, as nobody wants to take back what he or she cleaned out.

Used clothing patterns are appreciated, especially patterns for baby clothes since they are hardly used, as children's sizes change almost as fast as you can make an outfit.

Displaying Craft Projects

"What is this used for?" is a common question asked at a bazaar. I was once showing my decoupage boxes. A woman picked up each and every one of them and asked me to tell her exactly what she could use it for.

Aside from wanting familiar items, most people want to find a use for something before buying it. Part of good bazaar planning is determining the way the items will be displayed at the individual booths. The less explaining, the more sales appeal. If, for example, you display the decoupage trinket boxes on page 55 filled with various objects, it will suggest what the buyer can use them for. Try to be as creative in this area as you are in the creation of your projects. By showing one or two uses, you can then suggest others. Don't assume that the buyer will automatically figure a use out just because it seems obvious to you.

Remember, the people who come to the bazaar are looking at a lot of items. They are carrying these images with them even after they leave a booth. They may be thinking about the stuffed pillows and bookbinding projects they just saw as they approach your booth. Your job is to attract them to your projects in the most appealing way so they will remember them, even if they don't buy on the spot.

Present your items so that people respond to them in a positive way. It is always rewarding to have someone say, "That's a good idea. I'll take one."

When setting up your display, keep in mind that you are competing with the boutiques and department stores for the same dollars. Try to do what you can with the limitations you're faced with. Obviously you aren't setting up a boutique, but a good presentation can help sales.

If you are selling place mats, use accessories as props. Make one pretty setup with just the right napkin, a plate, perhaps silverware, and even a small bouquet of flowers or a wineglass. Or set everything up on a tray. This will serve as an example for the variety of place mats that you are showing and that are laid out for selection on a table.

However you choose to show the usefulness of your projects, make your demonstration example as attractive as possible. By concentrating on designing the single display, you won't feel overwhelmed with the prospect of figuring out how to display everything. Once people are attracted to your area, they can examine your craftsmanship, but first they must be interested enough to look.

Booth Displays

There are other considerations for displaying your projects. The overall appearance of the booth is important. If your bazaar has a theme, create a look that goes with it. This might be as simple as making a poster in Fourth of July colors. Or, if the theme is "Springtime," each booth might be adorned with a giant paper daisy and yellow cloth or paper table coverings. However, if each person is responsible for displaying his or her wares, your particular area should make a statement. If you've made baby items, for example, the display should be delicate and cute. Don't present the projects on an old card table.

If you have kitchen items, perhaps you can construct an environment that includes a backboard on which you hang potholders, aprons, etc. Cover a tabletop with white Con-Tact paper to look like Formica. Butcher block paper is also available. If you're selling containers for kitchen utensils, display them as you might in the kitchen. In other words, try to create a small area that suggests the theme of what you are selling. In this way each item relates to the others, rather than having to stand on its own.

There are lots of clever and inexpensive ways to display your projects. Look around in the five-and-ten, hardware, and houseware departments as well as novelty and card shops. Accordion wall hooks come in colors and cost very little. Folding clothes-drying racks are now made in colorful plastic and are ideal for display purposes. Giant pushpins are found in card stores and work well on a dark corkboard. Use ladders for display. Inexpensive hooks can be spray painted if color is needed. Hang large decorative shopping bags as well as the smaller, shiny ones. Fill each with a stuffed animal so that its head is showing well above the opening. When purchased, the package is part of the item, solving the problem of how to carry or give it as a gift.

Two of the largest craft fairs in the country are held in Baltimore, Maryland, and Rhinebeck, New York, each year. Approximately 350 craftspeople participate at each. The purpose of these fairs is to give craftspeople a chance to sell their work to wholesalers as well as to the general public. Because these people depend on this marketplace for 75 percent of their income, it is very important for them to display their work in the best way possible to attract buyers.

Some of them create an area made of pegboard and burlap, with the crafts displayed on card tables. Others make their booths look like a Madison Avenue showroom, complete with track lighting, glass exhibit cases, and very elaborate stands. If you have the opportunity to go to some fairs, look for ideas worth remembering. Jot down anything that will help you assemble your items. Look at store window displays with this in mind.

Since the idea is to have fun and to raise money, you don't want to design something that will cost a lot or take a lot of time and effort to construct. Keep in mind your capabilities, and try to be as realistic as possible. Establish your goals before plowing ahead. Do you have crafting skills that you can contribute, other than the obvious? Maybe you're good at lettering and drawing simple shapes which would be appropriate for a sign. Someone else might lend building skills in exchange for your poster expertise.

At one successful fair I attended, a potter had an appealing display for her hanging planters. Her husband created a simple structure of two-by-fours which looked like a grape arbor. The pots (some filled with plants) hung from the side trellises and from overhead. The table in front of her held the nonhanging pots. The structure was cut and planned at home and simply screwed together at the site.

Folding screens, chicken wire on a simple frame construction, and canvas panels are inexpensive and easy to make.

General Craft Tips

When you work on any craft project, it's helpful to go over the materials needed before starting. Each crafting technique will require different materials, but there are some things that you can't do without for all crafts:

1. Sharpened pencils
2. Pad for jotting down notes, measurements, time, cost
3. Straightedge and ruler
4. Tracing paper for transferring designs and making patterns
5. Sharp scissors for cutting fabric
6. Small embroidery or cuticle scissors for cutting thread, paper, trims
7. Newspapers
8. Craft knife such as X-Acto and single-edge razor blades

Sewing

Sewing projects are always the most popular at craft bazaars. They are also the most fun to make because everyone can contribute in some way. Even the untrained person can add trimmings or buttons to premade items. Because so many people sew, it's practical to solicit as much help as possible for the general cause.

Pooling Materials

Send out a general letter to all members of your group asking for scrap donations. You'll get a terrific variety of accumulated scrap fabric that is impossible to find in one sewing basket. Scraps can be used for many of the projects here, and the material you collect will inspire many others.

While such items as pins, needles, thread, buttons, snaps, hooks, and other notions are relatively inexpensive, the cost mounts up when you make items in quantity. If each person contributes a little here and there, such as used spools of thread or a remnant of decorative ribbon, it helps.

Cutting Out Patterns in Quantity

It is more efficient to make several items from one pattern. If you feel that the projects should be varied, do so by your choice of fabrics, colors, and trimmings.

Allow plenty of room for cutting. When possible, use a large tabletop. If you don't have one, it's easy enough to create by placing a hollow-core door or piece of plywood on two horses or sturdy step stools. If you must, use the floor, although this is the least desirable for comfort.

Simple patterns are the best for assembly-line sewing. Take time to study the pattern. If you are using one of the patterns from this book, trace it first, then transfer to plain paper. If it must be enlarged, refer to page 34.

Choose the fabrics, and lay one on top of the other. The number of layers to be cut at one time will depend on the type of fabric used. Be sure to have the bias of each going in the same direction. Take care when laying down printed fabric. You want to have the design come out right, not upside down. In the case of stripes, they should be straight up and down.

Pin all material together, and place the pattern on top. After the outline of the pattern is cut, each piece must be individually marked. This can be done with chalk. Mark notches on edges. For inside markings, insert pins through the pattern and fabric at intervals along lines. Fold the pattern back to the pins, mark both sides, and remove the pins.

If several people are working together, one might do all the cutting, another the marking and pinning, while still another presses each piece.

Tracing Patterns

Another way to cut patterns is: Cut a pattern from cardboard, and trace it as many times as possible on the back of the fabric, allowing for seams. When you use prints, it is most economical to select those with an overall pattern such as tiny flowers, polka dots, etc. In this way you can cut all the pieces on the grain, crosswise and lengthwise. For pieces that don't need patterns, such as squares and rectangles that are used for potholders, place mats, and napkins, it saves time to cut them out in long strips, to bind them, then to cut them apart.

Pressing

This is an important aspect to your sewing, as any good sewer knows. Have an ironing board set up near your sewing area. You will press your fabric at each step along the way. Press each seam or dart before you join it to another seam. Press with the grain of the fabric when possible.

Pinning

As each separate piece is pressed, someone else should be pinning correct pieces together for sewing. If you are working alone, do all the steps—cutting, marking, pressing, pinning, and sewing—for all pieces at once, rather than complete each item one at a time.

Place the fabric together as indicated for each pattern, and place pins up and down rather than horizontally. In this way the sewing machine runs over each pin without interference. The pins can then be removed after all sewing is completed. This saves a lot of time.

Finishing

If snaps, zippers, buttons, trim, or embroidery are to be added, plan each one carefully. Often this is the added detail that makes a project unique. Take the time to choose and plan placement. Sometimes an oversized button on a small change purse makes a difference. I used plastic bracelets, rather than the traditional small curtain rings, to hold the potholders. Beads, sequins, embroidery, lace—all add that boutique quality to ordinary items. Coordinate colors. Sometimes contrasting thread is all that is needed to add visual interest.

When the item is complete, press carefully and snip away any excess thread. The details count here. Check over each project to be sure it is neatly finished. You can also add your own sewn-in labels. See the Source List of Materials for where to order personalized labels.

Enlarging Patterns and Designs

Use a piece of graph paper large enough to accommodate your design, or draw your own grid to scale. For example, if the scale says "each square equals 1 inch," draw a grid of 1″ squares on your paper. Make sure you have the same number of squares on your grid as on the original. Copy the design in the book onto your grid one square at a time. For difficult designs, mark each grid line with a dot where it is intersected by the design. Then connect the dots following the contour of the original.

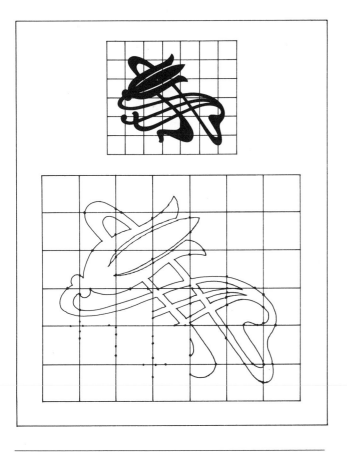

Transferring Designs

Trace the designs from the book or from your enlarged pattern. Use carbon paper and a sharp pencil to transfer the design to your material. Or you can turn your tracing paper over and retrace the design. Lay this on your fabric, and rub the pencil over the design outline, thus transferring it to the fabric. For felt or dark fabrics use dressmaker's carbon and a tracing wheel.

Painting

Whenever a project calls for painting, try to use spray paint for large items or painting in quantity. Acrylic paint is excellent for small things. It is fairly inexpensive, comes in every conceivable color, is available in small and large tubes, goes on like oil paint but cleans with water. It is also permanent on fabric. Spray and acrylic paints dry quickly and can be protected with Krylon clear spray varnish, which also dries in minutes.

New Products

Since so many people are crafting, many large manufacturers are developing their materials for the craft market. They may not have been in the craft business, but the introduction of a product opens up a new area of sales. For example, one company I wrote to sells satin sheets. It has remnants which it now packages in squares to be used for quilting and appliqué. A leather manufacturer in Connecticut packages scraps for the craft market. Some chemical companies have developed new fast-drying finishes for decoupage. Sewing aids are introduced often. Sometimes the new product is more expensive to use than doing it the old way, but often it can be an improvement on technique and help cut down on the time required. Look into this in relation to your specific craft by checking out the stores that normally carry your supplies. Read through the mail-order catalogs. The suppliers will tip you off to anything new and worth knowing about.

Familiar Projects with Pizazz

Several years ago I attended a bazaar and was attracted to one booth in particular. It was colorful, the sign was professionally lettered, and the items were tastefully displayed. But I couldn't tell what they were. People walked by, glanced, but didn't stop to look or buy. I had the same reaction, not wanting to take the time to find out what was being sold since other booths drew me on. This is the nature of a fair or bazaar.

Selling at a bazaar is based on impulse buying. People have come to find bargains, to satisfy their curiosity, to support a worthy cause, and to have some fun. Sometimes they expect to see the unusual but nothing so different as to be unrecognizable. If they appreciate handwork, they look for new designs applied to familiar items, and they look at the craftsmanship. Nobody is under obligation to buy. Since there is much to look at, we are rarely drawn to that which we can't identify.

There are many useful items that lend themselves to decoration. Often, browsing through a gift shop, we will find many new variations of common items. We pick up a simple china soap dish covered with rosebuds and remark, "Isn't this lovely?" Small dried-flower bouquets tastefully arranged in little baskets are appealing, even though we've seen them displayed in many different ways. Ordinary guest towels take on a whole new dimension with the addition of delicate ribbon trim or a satin appliqué.

Look through department stores, mail-order gift catalogs, a fine boutique for some ideas. By now we are getting used to the shocking prices, but many of these items (or a simpler version) can be made for a fraction of the cost.

Decorating standard inexpensive items is a wonderful way to express creativity. You will not spend a great deal of time making the items. Your input is concentrated on the decorative aspect. This might mean adding initials, appliqués, embroidery, stenciling, or decoupage to existing things. Once you've scanned the boutiques, check out the five-and-ten. Most of your basics can be found there, and the prices make them affordable for your purposes. They can be resold once you have given them some pizazz.

The following projects fall into this category. They are standard, useful, inexpensive, and have a high degree of appeal when decorated. The time and total cost to turn each into a bazaar item are small, making them quite desirable for profitable sales potential.

Ankle Art

Cotton ankle socks are the latest rage. No longer restricted to baby wear, ankle socks are taking a definite place in fashion, especially with teen-agers. Many boutiques carry them in fashionable colors of purple, pink, bright blue, fuchsia, and subtle shades of green, wine, etc. Some are simply dyed; others are decorated with beads, buttons, sequins, and appliqués. The more elaborate ones, and therefore the most expensive, are hand-painted. With the in-

troduction of fabric crayons and embroidery paint tubes it is easy to create a distinctive decoration.

Ankle socks are fun and easy to decorate and therefore open up an area of creative expression. They are least expensive from the five-and-dime but can also be found for only a few cents more in lingerie stores.

Before you begin, try to imagine who in your community would buy them. In this way you can plan how many to buy in different sizes. It is a good idea to plan for more infant and young girl's sizes. The tiny infant socks come in pastel colors, but I suggest buying all white. In this way you can create the more exciting colors that cannot be purchased.

Materials Needed

Several pairs of white cotton socks; a variety of buttons, sequins, appliqués, ribbons; fabric crayons, embroidery paint tubes, or similar materials for decoration; needle, thread, and scissors; a variety of Rit dyes and an iron.

Directions

The first step is to dye the socks. You will fill a bowl with hot water into which the dye is dissolved according to the package directions. However, to obtain different shades of one color, leave the socks soaking for different lengths of time. The longer they soak, the darker the shade. In this way you can economize by using fewer packages of dye. From Old Rose you will get a deep pink, a pastel pink, and a faded trace of color which is more interesting than a commercially dyed pink. Purple is a smashing color to work with. The deep color is vibrant and very intense, and you can then make other socks several shades lighter.

Dry all socks, and iron them before decorating. You can use your imagination when picking out the decorations. Rickrack, ribbon trimmings, and embroidered appliqués are the easiest to apply.

Variations

Fabric crayon designs enable you to create your own original hand-painted look. This is fun and a lot easier than it looks. Trace one of the designs

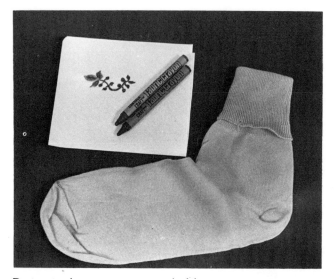

Design is drawn on paper with fabric crayons, creating an iron-on transfer

from the book or from any other source available to you. Color in the design on the paper with special fabric crayons, available in five-and-tens, art stores, and some fabric shops.

Set iron to cotton setting. Place a piece of scrap fabric or newspaper on the ironing board. Put the sock on this. Lay the crayon design facedown on the sock in the exact position where you want it to appear. Put a piece of plain paper or fabric on top, between the paper design and your iron. Press down with the hot iron in order to transfer the crayon design. Remove the top papers, and the design is set. Repeat on the other sock, making sure to use the right side, so the designs match and are on the outside of each ankle.

You can use this design over and over but you must recolor before ironing it down each time.

Embroidery paint tubes are made by Vogart and

38

Design is transferred to sock in preparation for coloring with fabric paint applicators

Plan the designs to be used so that all sewing decorations can be done at once. This is a good project to do during otherwise-wasted time—relaxing, waiting in a doctor's office, etc. If you are good at embroidery, consider using this method even though it takes extra time. Since each area to be adorned is small, this is a good place to put your talents.

These projects are perfect for doing at a social gathering. Everyone's input can be used. Take the time to collect a variety of materials. Everyone can bring something—a little ribbon, extra buttons, beads. You want a lot of variety, and it doesn't take any training to create designs.

Display Ideas

A clothesline makes the perfect display piece because it won't cost you much and each pair of socks can easily be shown. When doing your dyeing, throw the clothesline into one of the colors if you like.

To hold each sock, use painted clip-on wooden clothespins. Krylon spray paint comes in many colors and is fast-drying. Select colors to match the dyed socks as well as contrasting ones. The pins add to the overall look of gaiety and, if you like, can also be sold. Fill a basket with painted clothespins, and suggest them as reminder note holders for a desk.

are sold in art and craft stores and some fabric shops. The cherry designs were done using this method. Trace and transfer the desired design onto the socks. Place several layers of paper inside the sock under the area to be painted. Choose the colors you want, and apply the colors directly to the sock. The directions come with the tubes of paint, and it is as easy as writing with a marker. The effect is like thread embroidery. Once you get the feel for it, you can add shading and emphasize different areas by combining colors. This takes more time than the crayon method.

Making in Quantity

For efficiency do all dyeing at once. Decide how many of each color you will make, and put all socks into the dye of that color. Remove the ones that will be lighter in color as they are done.

Combs and Barrettes

Assemble hair combs, barrettes, bobby pins, and all the trimmings for a creative evening's fun. All that's necessary to turn a plastic comb into a smashing hair ornament is some ribbon, silk flowers, plastic berries, buttons, or beads and glue.

It takes minutes to create them, and almost anything goes. Wind embroidery thread, or yarn, around inexpensive plastic bracelets to match the combs. Or use clothesline. Cut the desired length, stitch the ends together, and wrap with ribbon or embroidery thread.

The butterflies on one of the combs are cut from wrapping paper. Bend the wings up, and glue the body to the comb. Coat each on the top and underside of wings with clear nail polish to stiffen and add shine. Two or three more coats will make them sturdier.

Decorative Soap

This is a good bazaar item because you can make enough in one day to fill an entire booth. Also, the cost is low, and the results look terrific. The items make up a colorful display, and the bonus is that you create a sweet-smelling area sure to attract attention from passersby.

If you want to combine this project with others, consider making decorative towels and other bathroom accessories. A suggestion for would-be customers: Tuck a bar of soap into a gift of lingerie, or give with a lacy handkerchief. If you are making these for yourself, they can be used for guests or given as small tokens. They make lovely stocking stuffers for Christmas, and a set of three can be gift boxed for a bride's shower or new-baby arrival.

Materials Needed

Bar of soap; decals, seals, or cutout paper designs from cards, wrapping paper, etc.; cuticle scissors and glue for paper other than decals; protective coating—clear varnish or paraffin when making several, clear nail polish if you're only making one.

Directions

Select soap that has a nice shape. Sweetheart soap has a design on it, and the oval shape is appealing. The easiest and quickest way to decorate the soap is with decals. These can be found in the five-and-ten, and the Meyercord Company (see Source List, page 171) has the greatest variety. Choose a design that will fit the surface of the soap. Once the decal is dry, protect with a coat of clear nail polish. In this way the soap can be used right down to a sliver as long as it isn't completely submerged in water.

Variations

Another method for designing the soap is the application of cutout paper motifs. These can be taken from greeting cards, wrapping paper, or similar sources. If you are making several items, this can be a money saver but takes a little more time.

Use cuticle scissors to cut out the desired designs, such as flowers, butterflies, bows, leaves, and shells. Glue an arrangement to each bar of soap. Pat down with a clean towel. While clear nail polish is a perfect quick-drying protective coating for one project, it is not practical for coating a quantity. It is

42

expensive and time-consuming. Consider one of two alternatives.

1. Melt a bar of paraffin wax in a pot on the stove. Paraffin is inexpensive and available in supermarkets. Set the burner on low. Use tongs to grasp each bar of soap. Quickly dip only the top surface into the hot wax, and remove immediately. The paper design will have a thin clear wax coating over it. Set each aside to dry for a few minutes. All the dipping should be done at once while the wax is hot.

2. The second method is the easier and quicker. Place all the bars of soap on waxed paper or a similar nonsticking surface, and spray the tops with Krylon clear varnish. Read the directions on the can for an even, accurate application. Varnish can also be applied with a brush. For this you will need a pint of indoor clear high-gloss varnish, a 1-inch brush, and brush cleaner. One coat is sufficient.

Making in Quantity

For efficiency two people should work together. Do all the cutting out of designs first. One person glues the designs in place while the other dips each bar as it is ready into the paraffin. Before you begin to dip, have approximately five bars ready.

If you are using the spray varnish method, you both can cut, arrange, and glue all the designs at once. When you have enough projects to make a display, varnish them all with one spraying. This should be done outdoors. With this much spraying at one time the fumes can be overpowering.

Display Ideas

A small and inexpensive item such as this should be dramatized in some way to give it a gift quality.

If the bars of soap are simply laid out on a table, they will be pretty but will not command the attention they could if each one is treated separately.

Place each bar of soap in the center of a piece of shocking pink tissue paper, and draw the tissue up around it. This will create a nesting package. Spread the tissue open so that the soap shows. In this way you can easily create a colorful booth that will attract people. At the same time you will discourage the handling of each bar, without having to say, "Please do not touch."

When a purchase is made, gather the tissue around the selected bar, and tie with a piece of yarn or ribbon. Have your ties already cut to the appropriate length. If you have a label for your bazaar, stick it onto the tissue, and your customer will have an instant gift package. This will enhance its appeal as a purchase.

Another suggestion is to show the soaps in a basket. Line it with a piece of satin, velvet, or lace, and set each piece of soap down. Tie a satin bow around the basket or to the handle. Add a few dried rosebuds or artificial flowers here and there. Several small baskets can be placed on a fabric-covered table. Keep the overall feeling light and delicate by using pastel colors and romantic prints or fabric.

If your specialty is painted soap dishes, this would be a natural combination of projects. Design the soap dish to match the soap, and tie each together with a half-inch satin ribbon. Tuck a small dried flower into each bow.

Baby Tees

Carter undershirts are plain white and come in several sizes and over-the-head or button-on-the-side styles. When decorated or brightly dyed, they can be taken out of the undershirt category and proudly worn out front. They make delightful summer shirts for your own baby or to be given as a gift.

Undershirts are relatively inexpensive and make good bazaar items. Whether they are displayed in use (hard to do unless you have a very cooperative baby who will model all day) or hanging or lying on a table, they always attract attention.

Materials Needed

Carter's baby undershirt; Rit dye in color of your choice (Purple and Old Rose used for these); satin ribbon or embroidery tape (for quantity, measure around seams of neck and arms and shoulders of the size you're working on); needle and thread; scissors; iron-on transfer number (sold in fabric stores) and an iron. For heart design: tracing paper; stencil paper; X-Acto knife; stencil brush; white acrylic paint.

Directions

Dye shirt according to directions on the package. Press the shirt once it is dry. The iron-on number is called PRO number and is sold on a sheet that includes different sizes and a complete alphabet as well. The colors available are red, white, and blue. Set your iron for cotton, center the number on the shirt, and iron it on. Peel away the paper backing, and presto! The transfer will be permanent, and the shirt can be machine washed, but should be hung to dry.

Use ¼-inch satin ribbon to trim the edging all around the shirt. This is easier to do by hand than on the machine. Just three steps, and you have transformed a plain undershirt into a couturier football shirt for someone who hasn't yet learned to walk.

Variations

Stenciled hearts

Dye the shirt. Trace the heart provided here, and transfer it to stencil paper. Cut the design out with an X-Acto knife. Decide where you will place the hearts. A random pattern will look just as good as one that is symmetrically planned.

Hold the stencil cutout firmly on the fabric. Fill in the area with white acrylic paint in this way: Use the stencil brush in a vertical position with the paint partially brushed off. The paint should go on the fabric almost dry.

To create this exact pattern, begin in the center of the neckband directly under the label. Work to the right and left of it. Place the diagonal band of hearts down the front and on the back, creating an impression of a continuous design front to back.

For other variations, use one of the illustrations provided here to make your stencil. Names can also be ironed on. It takes longer to do this, but it can be a terrific drawing card for a bazaar booth.

Making in Quantity

Do all dyeing of each color on a sunny day if possible. If the shirts are put in the dryer, allow for shrinkage when selecting sizes. Sew all trimmings at the same time. This goes for the iron-ons as well. Create his and her designs, which may only require changing the colors of dye, ribbon, or numbers.

Display Ideas

The photograph suggests an effective way to display the shirts so they can be seen. If you do use a clothesline, consider throwing it into one of the dye pots at the time of dyeing. The clothespins used to hold each shirt are brightly colored with spray paint.

Draft every eligible two-year-old member of your organization to wear a shirt during the day of the bazaar. Wherever they go, you will have free advertising.

Baby Tees   Stencil designs

Decorator Towels & Soap Holder

An ordinary hand or guest towel can be trimmed with beautiful ribbon, embroidered tape, a satin appliqué, or lace, and suddenly it's no longer ordinary. Have you priced these items in bath shops lately? For a fraction of the price your bathroom can be just as elegant as those shown in the showrooms, and these items are always a big seller at bazaars. Spend the time to choose your trims carefully. If you are trying to keep the cost low, you can always find inexpensive "seconds" of towels. Buy the better, plusher products if you are making them for yourself or feel you can sell them for more money.

Materials Needed

Towels; embroidered tape 1 inch longer than the width of the towel; needle and thread; scissors.

Directions

This is just a simple sewing project that can be run up on the machine or by hand. The only detail to be careful of is to sew the tape on straight. If there is no line to follow on the towel, use a strip of masking tape just above the area to be covered. This will give you a straight line without a pencil mark.

Variations

Satin and embroidered appliqués can be purchased ready-made in many sizes and styles. You can even buy monograms. Ribbons come in all different widths and prices, depending on how elaborate they are. A good notions store is the best place to decide how you will trim your towels. It is almost impossible to plan this at home without first seeing what is available.

Combine the ribbons that you have on hand with others that are more exciting in order to make wide bands of trim.

Soap Holder

The embroidered ribbon can match the towels, or you can use contrasting designs and colors. When matched, they can be used or sold as a set.

The ribbon must be long enough to go around two or three cakes of soap laid in a row and to be tacked together in between each cake. The width of the trim will be determined by the size of the soap you use.

Turn down both ends of ribbon about one inch on the top, and sew edges together. Sew a plastic ring to the top back, and hang on a bathroom hook. This will keep your bathroom smelling sweetly, and extra soap is always at hand.

Display Ideas

I like to see delicate or light-colored fabrics in a dark and textured container such as the basket shown here. Wood is also attractive, and if you have an old wooden chest, consider displaying your towels in this. If you will be displaying many items, consider lining an old trunk with fabric or paper (a large, old-fashioned tablecloth can be used, draped inside) and arranging your items in this.

There are also many inexpensive picnic baskets available, and best of all, baskets are a way of carrying everything to the bazaar and home again, if necessary. If it's possible to have a backboard setup, cover it with delicate paper, and hang the towel holders for display.

Ordinary cardboard gift boxes can be covered with a basket-weave paper (Wall-Tex vinyl miniature collection, for one). Make a boxed set of two towels and matching soap holder, and display in this way. Use small bars of soap for this idea.

Fabric Lunch Bag

This bag is patterned after a common brown paper bag. It will be helpful to know that these are the lines to follow. Make it reversible with contrasting fabric; then, if you wish, turn to p. 124, and make matching eyeglass cases.

It's a handy bag to take to the office, for holding sewing supplies, knitting, or your lunch. Fold it into your purse when not in use; then whip it out when shopping. It's great to have for picking up little essentials on your way home. Terrific for a beach carryall.

Materials Needed

2 pieces of coordinated fabric, each 12 x 20 inches; 2 strips of fabric, each 13 x 1½ inches; piece of cardboard 3¼ x 5¾ inches; needle and thread; scissors; measuring tape or ruler; shoe box; iron.

Directions

Turn 13-x-1½-inch fabric strips in ¼ inch on each side. Fold in half, so you have two strips 13 x ½ inches. These are the handles for your bag. Topstitch.

With the two large pieces of fabric right sides together, place the handles between them 3 inches from the side edge and 2½ inches from the center of the fabric. Sew along top ½ inch from edge. Open flat.

Turn seam allowance under ½ inch at top and bottom. Press. Fold so that the like fabrics have right sides together, and sew side seams. Press seam open, and pull the top half of the bag over the lining half. The outside fabric is now outside and the lining inside.

Slip the bag over a shoe box, leaving 2½ inches hanging over the bottom. Fold in sides A. Then

fold down top and bottom sides B. Hand sew closed. Remove shoe box. Slip cardboard into bottom of bag. This will create a stiff bottom so that the bag holds its shape and is sturdy.

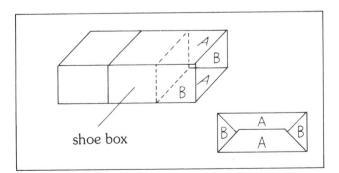

shoe box

Early Starters

While many bazaar crafts can be made quickly and easily, other best sellers take longer. Any of the traditional techniques that take time to master will have to be scheduled with this in mind. If you are planning to knit mittens and caps or sweaters, or if you are doing patchwork or needlepoint, you already know how long it takes to make one item. Plan how many you will need so you can start well in advance of the bazaar date.

Other projects require materials that must be planned for in advance. If, for example, you will be making anything with pressed flowers, you will need time to find and press them. You may have to collect flowers in the spring for projects that won't be made until winter.

Decoupage involves many steps of painting and varnishing, with more time for cutting and planning the designs. If you spread the work out over a long period of time, you will enjoy each process, create a number of items, and each object will vary in size and design. I have tried to eliminate any time-consuming projects so making decoupage items for bazaars can become feasible.

You should plan to make some of the larger sewing projects in quantity, and it may require teamwork in order to make enough to fill a booth.

Pressed-Rose Box

This project began in the form of a birthday gift of a bouquet of roses. It was February, and the roses reminded me of spring for almost a week. I hated to see them go, so just before they turned brown and died, I plucked the petals and pressed them. I was already pressing leaves from the fall—a crafter's lifelong, occupational habit!

The roses had already darkened from red to wine color, and I chose the leaves of the same color for my project. The box that I covered is made of wood, but you can find old metal recipe or cardboard boxes for this use. (See Source List for where to get wooden boxes.)

Materials Needed

Enough rose petals or other pressed flowers to cover a small box; Elmer's Glue-All; sponge; sponge brush applicator; razor blade; paint or paper or fabric for lining; Krylon clear spray varnish; piece of felt.

Directions

Press petals for at least a week. Sand the box. Dilute glue slightly with a few drops of water in a shallow dish. Spread glue over a small section of the box, using the sponge applicator. Place a few petals down, and pat in place with a damp sponge.

Continue to cover the box, adding glue where rose petals and leaves overlap. Cut and place pieces where the box needs filling in. If there are hinges or a catch on the box, work around them, but don't remove.

It takes a bit of time to cover the box completely, but the effect is that of a leather covering. When complete, spray varnish the entire surface. Let dry. Line or paint the inside, and spray with a protective coating of varnish. Continue to add coat after coat as each dries until the roses are embedded under varnish. This may take between five and ten coatings. Each dries in minutes.

Cut a piece of felt in a matching color to glue

51

onto the bottom of the box. This gives it a finished look.

Variations

If you are creating a pressed-flower collage, paint the box first. You can spray paint or use acrylic paint, which gives you more flexibility of color choice. Plan your design on paper before gluing each element in place. When making boxes at Christmastime, use pressed ferns on white backgrounds. A file box filled with holiday recipes is especially nice with one fern glued to the top and front. Paint the inside bright red.

Making in Quantity

If you decide to make more than one of these projects, be sure to press plenty of petals, leaves, etc., so you don't run out in the middle. It's hard to estimate exactly how much you'll need, so overdo it. Press some big leaves to use as filler for the backs of boxes in case you run short of the finer material.

To save time, create one design or illustration on a plain painted background. I made one box with the petals from one tulip. They were arranged in a semicircle over the top center of the box. The design looked like a sunburst. This was much easier to do than covering the entire surfaces.

Display Ideas

Cover a table with pretty, delicate fabric. If you can find a rosebud pattern, this might look nice as a background for the boxes. Arrange them at different heights for display. Clear Lucite pedestals or boxes are perfect. An alternative would be different-sized white gift boxes, or you could cover odd throwaways with white Con-Tact paper. Place each decoupage box on its own pedestal. This will create a nice visual display.

Another idea is to cover a surface with black velvet on which the boxes are arranged. Place small bouquets of the real flowers (when possible) beside each grouping of boxes. If you've used pressed rose petals, place a sprig of dried baby's breath next to each box for accent.

Pressed-Flower Bookmark

This is another project to start in the seasons when flowers can be picked for pressing. Only a few are needed for these bookmarks, and if you plan the design of each on paper, it will be easy to make many of them at once. Use a variety of leaves and petals.

Some flowers press better than others, and those that are small and delicate lend themselves best to the area that you'll be working on. Buttercups, pansies, daisy petals (not the centers or stems), Queen Anne's lace, and geranium petals can be pressed in the spring and summer. Sometimes I work with tulips, as the color and shape are especially nice.

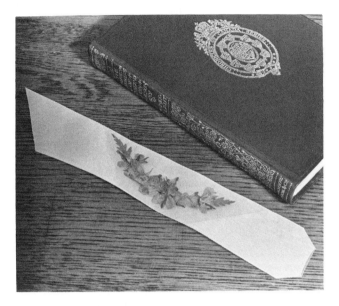

Materials Needed

Antique white satin ribbon 1½ inches wide by 9 inches long; an arrangement of pressed flowers; clear Con-Tact paper; scissors; tweezers.

Directions

Cut a strip of satin ribbon on the diagonal at one end. Cut the corners off the other end. Arrange pressed flowers on the ribbon. If they are delicate and difficult to pick up, use tweezers. Place them on the middle section of the ribbon.

Cut a piece of clear Con-Tact paper so that it fits over the pressed-flower section only. Press down to secure the flowers on the ribbon. That's it. A very pretty way to keep your place in a book. The perfect gift to give with a new book or the Paperback Book Cover on page 118.

Making in Quantity

This is a good project to make in quantity whether you repeat the design or do an original each time you make it. Begin by precutting all lengths of ribbon. You may want to use different colors for different arrangements. Mark and precut all pieces of Con-Tact, but don't peel the protective paper backing away from the adhesive until you are ready for each piece.

If you've pressed many of the same flowers and leaves, you can create one arrangement to be repeated until the flowers are used up. This will be the easiest. Make one finished bookmark to copy.

If you are working as a group, some people can arrange the flowers while the others adhere the Con-Tact.

Display Ideas

Slip each of these bookmarks into a clear plastic bag. If you have a label printed with your name or the name of your bazaar, stick it on the front. Lay each bag on a dark fabric-covered table.

Recipe File

This is another decoupage project that takes a bit longer than the trinket boxes but is not difficult to do. The file or recipe box that you use can be made of wood, metal, or cardboard, available in most stationery stores, although the wooden ones may be more difficult to find. (See Source List.)

The paper design that you select to cut out will determine how long the project will take. The more intricate the cutting, the longer it will take. A simple shape is best for a bazaar item. Each box can be lined with paper or painted and filled with recipe file cards.

Materials Needed

File box; acrylic paint; 1-inch brush; fine sandpaper; paper design to cut out; Elmer's Glue-All; sponge; cuticle scissors; Krylon clear spray or pint of indoor wood varnish (for which you will need brush cleaner); razor blade; furniture paste wax.

Directions

Paint the box. When it is dry, sand lightly. Cut out paper designs, and arrange on the box. Glue each element in place, and pat down with a damp sponge. This will remove excess glue. If the design overlaps the opening, cut across with a razor blade after gluing.

Apply several coats of clear varnish. If you are making just one box, use indoor wood varnish. Apply a coat to all exposed surfaces. Let this dry according to the directions on the can. Clean your brush between coatings. The long-drying canned varnish will give you a thicker, more appealing finish than the spray varnish, which has the advantage of drying quickly.

Sand lightly after three coats, and continue to sand between subsequent coatings of varnish.

Apply a coat of furniture wax to the finished project to give it a shine.

Variations

Use pressed flowers or silhouettes (see Source List) in place of the cutout paper designs. Designs cut from fabric can also be used, as can a photograph.

Making in Quantity

Make several of these as you would the trinket boxes described on the previous pages. If you are satisfied with the colors that Krylon spray paint comes in, this can save a lot of time. Use the spray varnish method as well. If you use the same few designs over and over, it will be easier as you can preselect those which require little cutting. In this way you can purchase a roll or sheets of wrapping paper that give you plenty to work with.

Display Ideas

See Pressed-Rose Box (page 50) for displaying boxes. Create a kitchen setting for recipe boxes, using simple utensils or objects.

Decoupage Trinket Boxes

Decoupage is an eighteenth-century craft of decorating a painted surface with cutout paper designs. Several coats of varnish are then applied to submerge the designs. A small box *usually* takes about ten days to make and is impractical for selling at a bazaar. However, there are many shortcuts that in no way make the results any less appealing. Since the cutting and drying time of the varnish makes this craft impractical, I've designed some projects that eliminate both. The technique, however, is the same, and the designs shown here are appropriate for the objects.

Small round boxes, which I have always called trinket boxes since I first began making them years and years ago, are great fun to design and have many uses. I work on a dozen at a time.

Materials Needed

Trinket boxes (see Source List); a variety of acrylic paint colors; a tube of white acrylic paint; 1-

55

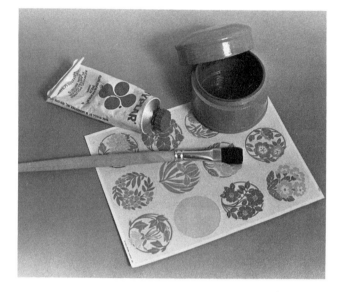

inch brush; fine sandpaper; Krylon clear spray varnish; paper seals such as Hallmark's (found in card shops, one package contains a variety of designs with several of each design for approximately $1).

Directions

Mix several different colors of paint to create a variety of pastels. You will need only a drop of color to four times as much white. Mix the paint thoroughly on a plate. The acrylic paint is easily washed off with hot water.

Paint as many boxes as you want in one color. The inside is painted a contrasting color. Let the paint dry. Sand the surface smooth and, if necessary, give each another coat of paint.

Select the paper seal that will go best with each background, and place in the center of the top. Be sure it is secure all around.

Spray coat after coat of clear varnish, allowing each to dry before applying the next. Five or six coats should be sufficient, and each coat will take approximately fifteen minutes to dry.

Variations

If the paper seals don't give you enough variety of design, you can create your own by cutting out flowers, butterflies, shells, etc., from wrapping paper, greeting cards, old book pages. Cuticle scissors will enable you to cut lacy designs easily. Arrange and attach these on the top, around and inside the box, with Elmer's glue.

Making in Quantity

Decoupage projects are well suited for a production line. It is satisfying to make one for your own use, but to sell, they are practical only when made in quantity. All the mixing and painting should be done during one work session. Decide how many you want to make, and have each person work with a different color so that the boxes will look good when displayed together.

The next step, which is sanding, takes awhile since each top must fit easily and the painted surface should be smooth. If working in a group, do all the painting on one day and the sanding and design application on another. The finished projects should be varnished inside and out, as well as the bottom. Give each box one spray coat of varnish and leave the rest of the varnishing until the next meeting. At this time you can decide if you want to move on to larger projects. (See Recipe File instructions, which precedes.)

Display Ideas

I always like to display my trinket boxes amid flowers, which is one way to display them. Fill the boxes with small items, such as rings, to show how they can be used.

Cricket Stool

I came upon this little stool in the five-and-ten. It's made of wood, is inexpensive, and is called a cricket stool. It's perfect for reaching out-of-the-way items on top shelves.

Any flat object like this or like a breadboard or a step stool is easy to work on and can be decoupaged, stenciled, or spray painted. If you can draw, use the oval shape to work with. A curled-up cat, a crouched rabbit, a ladybug, or a turtle can be painted on and protected with varnish. This one is done with decoupage. The art for the fence is provided here so that you can make one similar to it.

Materials Needed

Cricket stool (or wooden plaque); Krylon antique white spray paint; spray varnish; white bristol board (art supply store); floral greeting cards (with enough flowers to fill area); cuticle scissors; Elmer's Glue-All; sponge (to wipe away excess glue); fine sandpaper.

Directions

Sand all of the wood so that it's smooth. Spray all surfaces with antique white paint (or background color of your choice). Give it a second coat if needed. When this is dry, sand surface lightly.

Transfer the fence to bristol board, and add slats if necessary. The design provided here is the same size as needed for this project. No enlarging is necessary unless your project is larger than 9 x 13 inches, which is the size of the stool. Cut the fence out. Position it on the stool or plaque, but don't attach it.

Cut out paper flowers of a size appropriate for your project. These can be found on greeting cards and wrapping paper, in books, and on decoupage prints sold in craft shops. Arrange the flowers behind the fence before gluing each in position. Glue the fence over all. Make sure all edges are securely attached. Wipe off excess glue with sponge.

Spray several coats of varnish over the designs until they are sufficiently coated and the surface is smooth. Sand lightly, and spray one last time. Protect the legs with varnish as well. One or two coats are enough.

Variations

In addition to use for a bazaar item, this design can be adapted for the seat of a kitchen chair, the top of a bookcase, or a small dresser. The design works as well on kitchen cabinets.

Making in Quantity

Unless you find shortcuts, this project cannot be a profitable bazaar item. One suggestion: If you paint the background white and use flower designs that are printed on white, you won't have to do so much cutting. Lay the entire print or card down, and its background will blend in with the painted surface. Spray paint and spray varnish are a must. Decals can be used to cut down on time if necessary. This, of course, also limits design potential.

Display Ideas

If you make an item like this, you will probably have more than one design. Be sure to display them so that each one can be seen. If they're on a table, tilt each one toward the traffic flow.

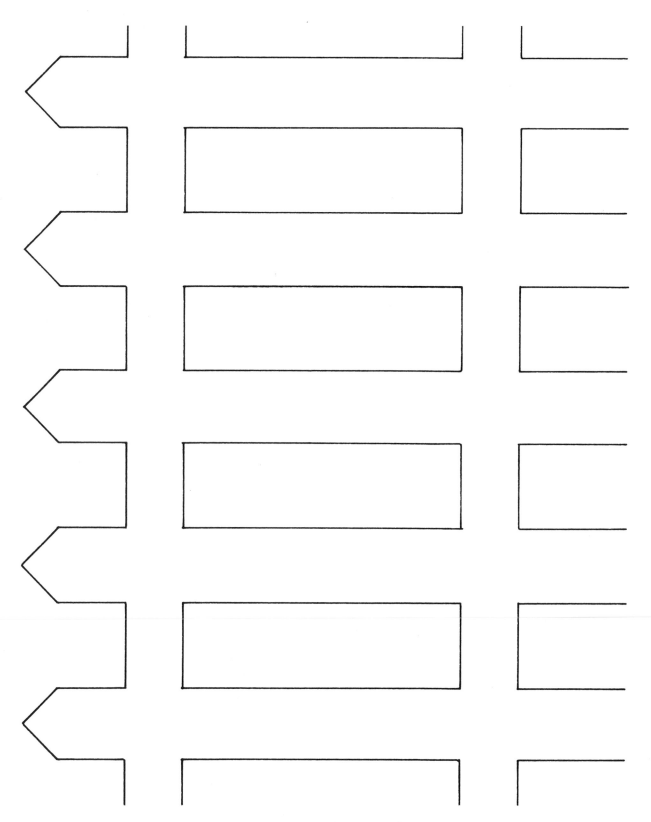

Natural Notes

Note cards made from bits of natural material will vary depending on where you live. My mother lives in Florida and designs cards with bits of sea grasses, a paper sandpiper, dried seaweed, sand, bark, and tiny shells. I like to use dried wild flowers, such as Queen Anne's lace (which presses better than anything I've used), buttercups, and rose petals. When living in Connecticut, I always collected and pressed leaves in the fall. Later they were used for many crafting projects such as this.

When you have the materials prepared, it is fun to design a group of cards. The nature of the material dictates that no two are exactly alike.

Materials Needed

An assortment of dried grasses, flowers, bark, (whatever you can find); white drawing paper; envelopes; scissors; ruler; pencil; white glue; tweezers; clear Con-Tact or plastic wrap.

Directions

You can make the cards all different sizes. However, be sure there are envelopes available before cutting the paper. This may determine the size card you make. White drawing paper has a nice quality for use as a greeting card.

Measure and cut the piece so that when folded it is the size you want. These are 4 x 6 inches.

Attach the materials with a small amount of glue. For a beach theme spread glue in an uneven strip along the bottom of the card, and sprinkle sand onto it. Shake off excess.

Tweezers will help you lift and place delicate pressed leaves and grass blades. The placement of the material is arbitrary.

Use a piece of clear Con-Tact paper to protect the front of the card. Or wrap each one in a piece of plastic wrap (Saran holds best).

Variations

Make Christmas cards with simple shapes cut from felt. Almost all five-and-tens and fabric shops carry an assortment of 9-x-9-inch pieces of felt. Pressed ferns on a white background suggest the holidays. Write a message with red marker.

For birthday cards, use the flower of the month. If you can't pick the flowers, buy what you need from a florist. Remember, one rose can yield enough petals for several cards, so it isn't necessarily expensive.

Making in Quantity

Gather, press, dry all materials. Decide how many cards each grouping will yield. Create a few basic designs, and repeat them often. In this way you can spend the time composing a few good layouts that will work with all the elements. It will be fun to design the first few, but it can be an overwhelming challenge if you feel that each must be unique. Of course, they will vary slightly from one to the other.

Display Ideas

Put each card in a small clear bag, and attach your personal label to one corner or the back of each card. (See Source List for printed labels.) A shallow square or rectangular basket or pretty box is a good way to display cards. Stand them up one behind the other so that the basket is full.

If you have a selection of designs, use one of each as an open display, but sell them from the basket. Write a greeting in each of the cards on display, and stand them on a table or shelf. People like to handle merchandise, so you must resign yourself to the fact that these may get soiled, but you are really using them to sell from. Have the envelopes visible so the customer can see that the card comes ready to send.

To display cards with a beach theme, fill a shallow box with sand and arrange the cards so they are standing in it. Scatter a few shells here and there. A dish garden might suffice in the same way for displaying pressed-flower cards.

Baby Carrier

Influenced by the Indian papoose carrier, this baby tote is one of the best products to be adapted for modern use by parents of small children. Since this item will carry precious cargo, use strong fabric, such as denim, corduroy, mattress ticking, etc. It can be made of double fabric so that it's reversible. When one side gets dirty, flip it over. Or make one side for everyday use, the other for partying.

Materials Needed

1½ yards of 45-inch-wide fabric; scissors; tape measure or ruler; needle and thread.

Directions

If you are making a patchwork motif, as shown here, use scraps of matching fabric, and cut sixteen squares, each 2½ x 2½ inches. Sew them together with ¼-inch seams to create a finished square of 8 x 8 inches. Press seams open.

Cut one background square 17½ x 17½ inches. Cut two pieces 17½ x 4½, and cut two pieces 8¾ x 5½ inches. These will be the borders of the patchwork square. Center one side border (17½ x 4½) on the patchwork square with right sides together, and stitch ¼-inch seam within ¼ inch of top and bottom of patchwork square. Do the same with the other side border. Press to right side.

Pin top border (8¾ x 5½) to patchwork square with right sides together. Sew ¼-inch seam up to side of borders. Do the same with remaining, bottom border. Fit under side borders, and topstitch all around. Lock all seams by backstitching at ends.

Place large back square on top of back patchwork square with right sides together. Sew all but one side together, leaving 2¼-inch opening at each corner. Turn to right side. Fold ¼-inch seam allowance in at open side.

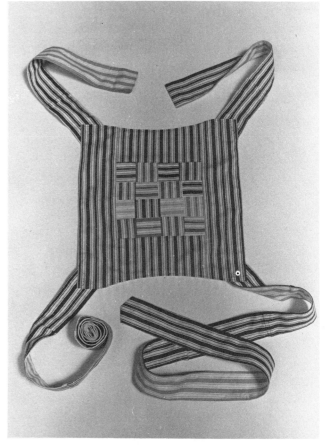

Baby tote holds baby in front or in back.

Fold in ¼ inch on all sides of the strap strips. Fold the material so that you have four straps 3 inches wide. Topstitch all around.

Insert a strap at each corner of the square. The short straps go on the bottom for the waist, and the long straps are attached at the top to go over shoulders. Pin in place. Topstitch all around the square, at the same time closing the open end, or bottom.

Stitch a triangle pattern at each corner to make the straps very secure.

Variations

The front and back pieces can be cut from the same material, and the patchwork square can be made separately and attached to the back. If you do this, stitch it to the back piece on the sides and bottom of the patchwork. Turn the top edge in to form a hem, but do not attach to the back fabric. This will create a handy pocket into which you can place an extra diaper, Handi Wipe, or other flat essentials. Consider decorating with embroidery or appliqué.

Making in Quantity

Gather all scraps, and make the patchwork squares all at once. In this way you will have a variety of decorative pieces to which you can attach any material to go with them.

Display Ideas

Baby totes almost have to be seen in use to be appreciated. However, the more colorful the designs and material used, the better the display. Whatever your crafting specialty, you can do it on this item—stencil, patchwork, embroidery, appliqué, silk screen—you can create an effect simply by using lovely material. Hang them all. Seeing them almost makes one want to have a baby. If you don't have a baby for modeling, take a photograph of it in use, have it enlarged, and use it for your display.

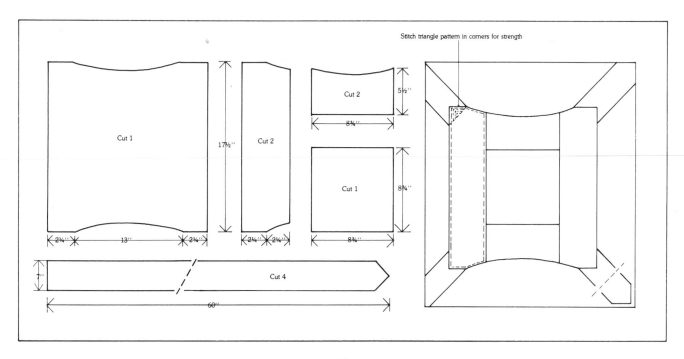

There are some projects that can best be done in a workshop environment. They may require some preparation time, or there may be many steps involved, or it is just more practical to put materials and multiple talent together. Book pad binding is a craft that is good to do in a group. There are many cutting and pasting steps, and a group can turn out a whole bunch of pads for a display very quickly. Everyone is involved in his or her step, making the overall process efficient. The group effort creates a social affair.

Cosmetic Bow Box

This little fabric box is versatile and sturdy because it is lined with mat board. You can make it in sets of three different sizes and, depending on its use, with all different fabrics. The first time I saw some they were made of red, yellow, and blue calico. But I was more interested in making them when I saw them again in a shopwindow. The entire space was filled with bow boxes made from elegant cotton French prints, and they were selling for $20 apiece.

If you already have enough fabric left over from other projects, to make these boxes will cost you nothing. If you make them with calico, you can produce a set of three for $7, and if you use very elegant fabric, it will cost you a bit more. The cost will be determined by your taste in fabric. For bazaar crafting, I would say try to find the nicest material you can for the least amount of money. Inexpensive materials have attractive colors, textures, and patterns, too.

Materials Needed

For a 5½-inch square box: 2 pieces of fabric 1¼ x 18 inches; 2 pieces of fabric 11 x 11 inches; 5 pieces of mat board: 1 piece 5½ x 5½, 4 pieces 2⅛ x 5½ inches.

Directions

Press hems of long strips ¼ inch along 18-inch sides. Fold in half, and topstitch so you have two strips 18 x ⅜ inches. Cut in half, and cut in half again. You now have eight ties ⅜ x 4½ inches.

Fold ½-inch hem down on all sides of the two 11-x-11-inch pieces. With right sides out, pin the two pieces of fabric together at each corner. Pin the ends of ties on right side of fabric at each dot on the pattern. Topstitch close to edge around three sides and through the ties on the fourth side. Leave open on the fourth side between ties.

Slip the mat boards (four pieces of the same size) into the pockets, leaving space between board

to stitch. Stitch, and then slip mat board number 5 into place. Stitch opening on fourth side.

Tie at each corner to form a tray.

Variations

You can make this project with two contrasting fabrics so that it becomes reversible or design it in different sizes to fit your needs.

Letter Tray

Directions are the same, but you will need the following material: 2 pieces of fabric 1¼ x 18 inches; 2 pieces of fabric 9½ x 15½; piece of mat board 4 x 10 inches; 2 pieces of mat board 2⅛ x 10 inches; 2 pieces of mat board 2⅛ x 4 inches.

Making in Quantity

When buying the mat board, have the number of strips you will need in each size cut at the art store on the paper cutter. This will ensure accuracy and save an enormous amount of time.

Display Ideas

The variety of fabrics will create the display. Completely cover a tabletop with the trays. Put some soap bars in one, letters in another. You won't have to do much to suggest their uses.

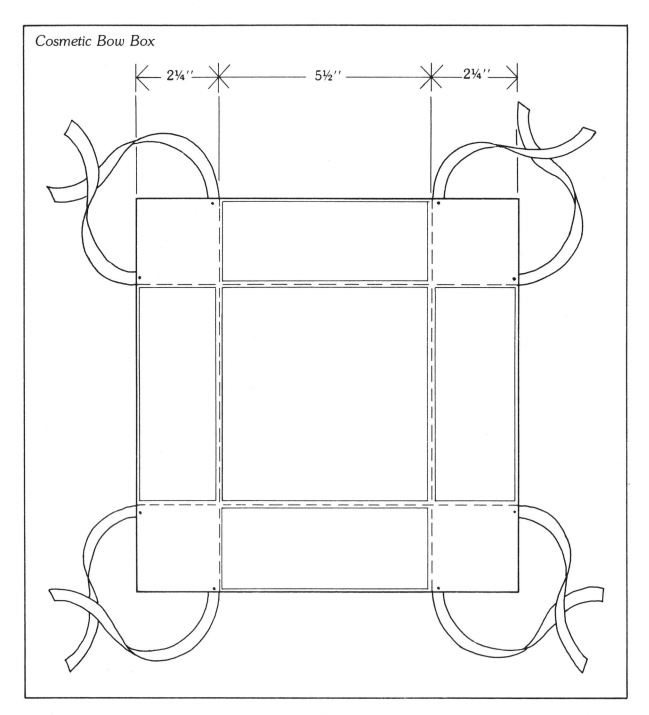

Cosmetic Bow Box

2¼'' — 5½'' — 2¼''

Photo Album Cover

Since everyone is taking pictures and has more than he or she can frame, photo albums are quite popular. These directions can be adapted for notebook or telephone covers as well. The album shown here matches the letter box on pg. 64.

Materials Needed

Plastic photo inserts 11¼ x 9 inches; two pieces of 9½-x-11¾-inch mat board; two pieces of 1¼-x-11¾-inch mat board; two pieces of fabric 13 x 15 inches; two pieces of fabric 8½ x 11 inches; one piece of fabric 5 x 14 inches; five pages of blank newsprint pad approximately 12 x 18 inches or larger (art supply store); fabric spray adhesive, such as Spra-Ment; scissors; craft knife; paper fasteners.

Directions

Lay two pages of blank newsprint on a flat surface. Spray fabric adhesive over the papers, and mount the 13-x-15-inch pieces of fabric on them, right side up. Smooth carefully. Use a rolling pin if necessary. Put aside to dry.

Cut the 5-x-14-inch fabric in half so you have two 2½-x-14-inch pieces. Cover one side of the smaller pieces of mat board with these two strips of fabric. Fold and glue excess fabric to opposite side.

To make the front and back of the album, place one piece of 13-x-15-inch fabric face down with the paper side up. Apply adhesive to the paper. Mount large piece of mat board in position (see diagram). Mount the fabric-covered strip of mat board next to the mat board, leaving a ¼-inch space as shown in diagram. Repeat this process with the matching pieces.

Fold the fabric down to cover three sides of the large mat board, and trim the fourth side at the edge. Mount the 8½-x-11-inch fabric on the inside

of the cover in order to cover all exposed mat board. Do this with the corresponding piece.

Make holes through the narrow strips that correspond to the holes in the photo inserts. The photo inserts are to be sandwiched between the narrow strips of fabric-covered mat board and held together with paper fasteners.

Making in Quantity

Have all mat board strips cut at the art store. They will make accurate cuts with the paper cutter.

Display Ideas

Select fabrics that relate in color or design. The fabric might also suggest the kind of photographs to be placed in the album. For example, a delicate rosebud print can be used for a baby album or a moire fabric for a wedding album.

Stenciled Boxes

The designs that have been created for your use fit on wooden boxes between 5 and 8 inches. Each one takes a few minutes to apply, and the decorative boxes that result go together to make up a nice display. The most time-consuming part of this project is cutting the stencils. This is really the only way to have original designs. However, if you want to use precut stencils, you can find them in art supply stores or craft shops, or see the Source List at the back of the book.

Stenciling is done with a special stencil brush held in a vertical position over the cutaway areas of the stencil paper. The paint is applied to these areas by tapping the brush up and down onto the surface you are working on. When the stencil sheet is removed, the design is accurately positioned with clean, sharp, well-defined edges.

Stenciling has become quite popular as a way of decorating furniture, floors, and even walls. The small boxes are feasible for a bazaar and will be appreciated by those who are familiar with the craft.

If you are selling these boxes, the price should be determined by the intricacy of the design. It will take additional time and effort to create designs with more detail.

Materials Needed

Hinged wooden boxes; tracing paper; stencil paper (available in art stores); a variety of acrylic paints; 1-inch paintbrush; X-Acto knife; stencil brush; Krylon clear spray varnish; small piece of felt (optional).

Directions

Tomato Recipe File

Paint the box inside and out. Set aside to dry. A separate stencil is used for each color in the design. This design uses two colors, one for the leaves and one for the tomato. To prepare the stencil, trace the entire design on tracing paper. Then transfer the leaves to one piece of stencil paper, and transfer the tomato design to another piece. Cut each transferred design out with an X-Acto craft knife.

Squirt a small amount of paint onto a flat dish. Tap the stencil brush on the paint, and then tap on newspaper a few times to remove excess paint. The paint should go on almost dry. Little paint is needed for doing this box and should be mixed as needed.

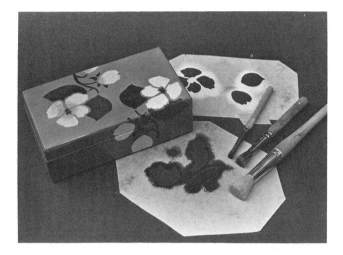

Place the tracing in the desired position on the box. Lay the stencil of the tomato over it, and carefully remove the tracing paper. Tape the stencil in position on the box.

Hold the stencil paper flat with one hand. In the other, hold the brush perpendicular to the surface with your elbow firmly positioned on the table. Tap the color onto the area.

When the first color is dry (takes minutes), replace the tracing in position as a guide for registering the second stencil. Place the second stencil over the tracing, remove the tracing paper, and tape the stencil down. Stencil the leaves onto the box. Complete stenciling of the second color by positioning the stencil so it will continue smoothly.

When the paint is completely dry, apply three or four coats of spray varnish to all sides. To finish off the box, place a piece of felt on the bottom.

Cut and stencil the other designs in the same way.

Variations

If you are creating a booth of stenciled boxes, consider cutting one design to be used on different-sized boxes that have been painted with different colors. Or choose one box, such as a recipe file, and create three or four designs to be used.

Since acrylic paint takes well to fabric, you can make matching potholders and aprons with the same stencil designs. The process is the same.

Making in Quantity

Stenciling is a perfect technique for doing things in quantity. If you set up a workshop of four people, one person paints the box, the second person stencils the first color, the third person stencils the second color, and the fourth person varnishes all boxes. When one set of stencils wears out, cut a different design for a different box. In this way you will create variety for your booth. The stencil usually wears out when you are tired of working on the same design over and over.

Note: If you cut one shape and use only one color, the time and work can be cut in half.

Display Ideas

Take one of the designs, such as the tomato, and stencil it all over a piece of white fabric to be used as a backdrop.

Note Pad Binding

This little item is a proved best seller at bazaars. Each one can be made up in a different color and pattern as the design comes from the paper that you use. Make them in different sizes for various uses. Everyone can use a pad, and these look very gifty.

At one of the fairs I attended there was a booth filled with bound note pads. As soon as the fair started, a crowd gathered around this booth, and by the end of the day it was the same. There had been a steady stream of people buying, yet the booth remained filled with a good selection.

I talked to the woman in charge, who told me that four women had spent months making these pads. She sold out wherever she showed them. The prices were right. One box was filled with small pads for $1. That was the drawing card. Who can pass up a pretty note pad for $1? The highest price was $3, and the seller was making a nice profit because she and her group had figured out how to make the pads quickly by working together.

Materials Needed

For a 3-x-5-inch pad: plain white pads available in stationery stores and purchasable by the dozen; Elmer's glue; 2 pieces of mat board 3¼ x 5½ inches; 1 piece of mat board ¼ inch x 5½ inches for single pad binder (you can make double pads also, for which you will need ⅝ x 5½ inches); 2 pieces of decorative paper (use folded, not rolled, gift wrap, wallpaper, or dollhouse wallpaper) 3¼ x 6½ inches; 1 piece of book cloth 1¼ x 6⅜ inches for the outer spine; 1 piece of book cloth 1¼ x 5 inches for inner spine (art store); white lining (bond) paper 2⅞ x 5 inches if using one pad; 1 piece of white paper 6¾ x 4¾ inches (cut 2 if using

2 pads; also note: The sizes of the above pieces can be changed to accommodate the size of your pads if they are different); straightedge and razor blade for cutting.

Directions

Note: This project sounds more difficult than it is. In reality it doesn't take a lot of time. The photographs should help you. The directions are here to refer to. If you read them before starting, you'll become discouraged.

Apply glue to the outer spine cloth, and place the mat boards on it, leaving ⅛-inch space between spine and cover boards.

Turn ends of spine cloth to inside. Glue inner spine cloth over outer spine on the inside. (Refer to photos.) Close booklet cover, and turn so the closed end is away from you.

Place decorative cover so that it overlaps the spine. Cut the corners close to, but not to, the corner. Apply glue and fold the edges in. Do the same on the back.

Glue smaller lining paper inside front cover (if using one pad). Slip paper for other pad pocket under the cardboard at the back of pad, and fold over to form a pocket. Glue the long edge and seal, making sure the pad can slip in and out easily. Apply glue to the folded side of pocket within ¼ inch of edges. Slip pocket (with pad) into binding, making sure to push the pad close to the spine, and even the margins at top and bottom. Place under a heavy book for about fifteen minutes until dry.

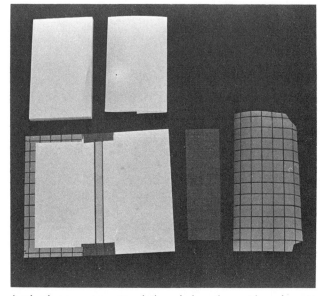

Apply glue to outer spine cloth and place the mat boards on it, leaving ⅛-inch space between spine and cover boards. Turn ends of spine cloth to inside. Glue inner spine cloth over outer spine cloth on the inside.

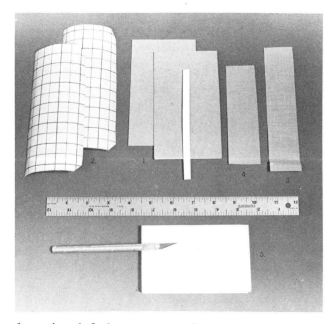

1. mat boards 2. decorative paper 3. book cloth (outer spine) 4. book cloth (inner spine) 5. lining paper

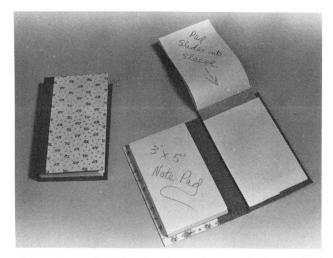

Note pads are held in place by pockets made from folded bond paper glued on inside covers, thus providing easy replacement.

Velvet Tote Bags

What could be more romantic than velvet, satin, and lace? If you enjoy making small sewing projects, consider these versatile bags. They have been designed for evening wear and are small. Select a good quality fabric (since the items are small, the extra expense isn't much), and plan the appliqués carefully. Velvet comes in 54-inch widths, and you will need only ¼ yard for each bag. If you can find remnants of velvet and satin, it will save you money.

Materials Needed

¼ yard of velvet, ¼ yard of satin; thread in same or contrasting color; tracing paper; small piece of heavy paper, such as oaktag, sandpaper, for making appliqué template; scissors; ruler or measuring tape.

Directions

Cut two pieces of velvet 6½ x 9½ inches. Cut two pieces of satin same size for lining. Cut a strip

of velvet 2½ x 36 inches long for handle.

With right sides pinned together, sew the two pieces of velvet along the sides and bottom, but not along the top. Do the same with the lining. Turn the velvet to the right side. Fold top hem ½ inch down toward the inside. Turn the top edge of the lining to the outside, forming a hem on the wrong side. Slip the lining inside velvet.

Make the handle by turning the long edges in to make a hem, and press. Fold the strip in half with wrong sides together. Topstitch closed so you have a strip 1 x 36 inches.

Pin the handle between the velvet and the lining at the side seams. Pin top of bag to lining all around, and stitch together. Secure the handles at each side with extra stitching to allow for the weight of carrying a full bag.

Applying Appliqué

The technique of appliqué is to lay pieces cut from one fabric onto another fabric and sew them in place. Trace and transfer one of the designs provided here to a piece of heavy paper such as oaktag or sandpaper. Cut this out to use as a template for the appliqué.

Place the template on the wrong side of satin fabric, and cut it out ¼ inch larger than the actual size. Press back the seam allowances over the pattern, thus making a distinct and accurate guideline for sewing. Clip the seam allowance to the marked design where necessary.

Remove the template, and pin the appliqué to the bag. Hand stitch all around edges, attaching it to the velvet. Stitch where details are indicated. If you prefer, you can stitch the details on the machine before attaching the appliqué to the bag. (See rose and shell motif.) Turn bag inside out, and press.

If you are using the swan design, detail is added with embroidery floss. For a subtle effect use same color thread as satin. For contrast use darker thread on pastel satin.

Variations

These bags can be made with a variety of fabrics, depending on how they will be used. For solid fabric use a printed lining, and vice versa. The handle can also be solid on one side, printed on the other.

Making in Quantity

Use the template to trace the number of shapes for each design you will need for the number of bags being made. You can cut three or four thicknesses of the satin at one time. The fabric slips, so pin all layers together before cutting. Trace the shapes onto the wrong side of the fabric, leaving ½ inch between each shape to allow for ¼-inch seams when cutting.

Display Ideas

When displaying these bags, stuff each with tissue paper so they appear full. Place a lacy handkerchief in one or two, and hang them from a pegboard. The background should contrast nicely with the colors of the bags. If you use dark velvet, the background can be covered with a light paper or piece of satin to match one of the appliqués. A lace tablecloth would also set them off in an attractive way.

Patchwork Pillows

In the past ten years there has been such a profusion of pillows that there is hardly a home without a few here and there. For a crafter, this is the ideal project. Who can't use one more pillow? Or a change of accents? The pillow gives us the canvas on which to create designs with needles, needlepoint and patchwork being the most popular. The following are two that are familiar and often selected when a group gets together to work. The beauty of the designs calls for an assortment of material, which comes from the variety of contributions.

Dresden Plate

For a 15-inch-square pillow: Use the pattern to cut out twenty petals of assorted colors and a piece for the center. Sew the edges of the petals together. Press seams open. Turn in around the outside scalloped edge, press down, and place in the center of a 16-inch square of unbleached muslin. Topstitch the petals down. Turn the edges of the center piece, and stitch it to the center of the petals.

Pin a 16-inch-square piece of matching muslin to the front of the pattern, and stitch up on three sides. Turn right side out, and finish off top hem. Fill with a polyfoam pillow or shredded foam rubber. Add zipper or snaps to closure.

Honeybee

This design combines piecing and appliqué. The pattern is for a 13½-inch-square pillow. There are all kinds of design possibilities here. You can use two contrasting fabrics or a solid for the squares and a print for the wings (as shown) or a combination of colors and patterns. This one is done in navy and pastel blues on white unbleached muslin. The fabric on the back of the pillow is the same as that used on the front.

Cut out the pieces according to the pattern. Place them on your fabric background as indicated. Pin each piece in place, and whip- or blind-stitch to the muslin. Quilt the front with cotton batting and another piece of muslin before sewing it to the back piece to create the pillow cover. Fill, and finish off the top edge with snaps or a zipper.

Display Ideas

Create an Early American booth of rustic wood to serve as the background for these designs. They will look especially nice in a large wicker basket, piled on a wicker chair, or arranged in a small open trunk. Line the trunk with old-fashioned wallpaper, even if it will only be partially seen. Tie a pretty ribbon around each pillow if it won't detract from the design. The pillows should be accessible, but not so they can be constantly handled.

Honey Bee Design

Dresden Plate Design

Satin Evening Bags

These little bags, used for evening wear, are very expensive to buy, and they look it. The satin material gives them an elegant quality, and because they are small, they needn't cost much to make. These are made from 5-inch-wide satin ribbon. If you can find blanket binding, use it. Otherwise, use satin fabric, which comes in many pastel colors. The size of the bag is perfect for holding a comb, a compact, and a few other small accessories.

Materials Needed

Satin ribbon 16 inches long by 5 inches; if you use satin fabric, allow ¼ yard for each bag; needle and thread; scissors; crocheted medallion, embroidered ribbon, or lace; snap for closure; 36 inches of braided cord for shoulder strap, if desired.

Directions

Cut two pieces of satin 17 inches long by 6 inches wide. Sew right sides together on three sides, leaving one of the 6-inch ends open. Turn right side out.

Fringe the open edge 2 inches from the bottom. Turn the *unfringed* end under, and topstitch. Fold the unfringed end up 4 inches to the underside. Topstitch on each side to make pocket pouch.

Fold fringed end down so that the fringe hangs down over the bottom of the bag edge (see drawings). Determine where the snap should be placed, and sew each half to the top and bottom.

Trim with a crocheted medallion, a piece of old lace, embroidered ribbon, etc. If you want to add a braided shoulder strap, black silk cord is available where ribbons are sold. Attach to either side.

Variations

These can be made in cotton and quilted for everyday use, or made in velvet as an alternative to satin. Since these are small, they are perfect for patchwork designs. Use muslin for the background, and pad it for a puffy bag.

Making in Quantity

Assemble all materials. Pin together as many layers of satin as you can cut through. Measure and draw the rectangle for the bag on the satin. Cut out all the bags at once. Sew up all seams, and press. Determine the designs for each bag. If you aren't using one-of-a-kind trim, establish three or four different designs, and stick with them. When too much variety is offered, people often have a hard time deciding and buy nothing. However, you don't want to limit your sales by presenting only one or two to choose from. With three or four designs, you will have a chance to see which sell best so you can plan accordingly for your next bazaar. Try different crafting techniques for each. Embroider one bag (see Embroidery Tips). Make an appliqué for another. Decorate with fabric crayons or embroidery ink (Vogart, available in art supply stores). Do patchwork on another.

If you're making bags for children, try felt shapes and clown faces made of yarn. Needlepoint a simple shape with cross-stitch. Use gingham fabric, and create the designs within the squares.

Display Ideas

To display the evening bags, stuff each with tissue paper or a hankie to give it a full look. For the simplest display, cover a table with pale satin material. Create folds, and gently place each bag down so that it is softly surrounded by fabric. This will encourage looking rather than touching.

If you can use a backboard, cover it with dark velvet and hang each bag for a dramatic effect. The contrast of pastel satin and dark velvet will make a striking display. Create an equally appropriate setting for patchwork or calico bags.

Overdoing a Good Thing

Some items are so familiar that they almost seem too ordinary to create for a bazaar. These are useful products and for this reason deserve consideration. But you'll have to use your imagination to make them better, brighter, prettier, cleverer, or in some way appealing enough to attract sales.

Potholders can easily go unnoticed. "I can get those anytime. I'll make them myself," people say. You've said it yourself. Or you've seen some elaborate ones, but they cost more than you think potholders should cost, no matter how cute they are.

Don't use remnants. No scraps here! No little squares. Think bold. Pick a color scheme, and really overdo it. Select patterns in your colors. Have some fun. Buy a quarter yard of every red and white cotton fabric in the store. Think Display. Don't save on material. If most potholders are 6 or 7 inches square, make yours 9 inches. Make large mitts to fit a man's hand. Big hearts are happy shapes. Make a lot. Make them striped, polka-dotted, checked, covered with little hearts, apples. Make them solid red. Get the idea?

Quilted Potholders

Choose a fabric with a repeat or geometric pattern. Cut two squares of fabric 10 x 10 inches and one square of polyester batting 9 x 9 inches. Turn the fabric in ½ inch on all sides, so you have two 9-inch squares. Put the batting between the front and back pieces of fabric. Topstitch the three pieces together. Cut a ribbon loop, and sew onto one corner. Machine-quilt by stitching between each design, either in squares or diamonds according to the print.

Panhandling

Cut a piece of fabric 6 x 14 inches, a piece of polyester batting 5 x 6½ inches, and a piece of ⅝-inch ribbon 5 inches long.

Press a ½-inch hem all around the fabric. Fold so it measures 5 x 6½ inches. Place batting between layers, ribbon at the corner, and topstitch all around. Quilt in square or diamond pattern. Fold so the holder measures 6½ x 2½ inches. Topstitch long edge and bottom.

Pot Mitt

Use a border print fabric for this. Enlarge the pattern, and cut it out, leaving a wide margin. Make it large enough to fit a man's hand, about 7½ x 10 inches. It will fit either hand.

Cut two pieces for the outside and two pieces for the lining. Turn under ¼ inch all around for seam allowance. Cut two pieces the same size for the batting.

Sew a piece of batting between one lining and one outer piece. Repeat. Use your fabric pattern as a guide, and quilt each half of the mitt.

With right sides to the outside, sew around the mitt edge, being sure to leave the bottom open for your hand. Stitch a loop of grosgrain ribbon to one side.

Heart to Heart

Cut two heart-shaped pieces 10 inches across and up and down (enlarge pattern). Cut a heart-shaped piece of cotton batting slightly smaller. Place batting between the fabric. Turn edges in ¼ inch all around. Topstitch by hand, or run this up on the machine. Quilt as above.

Potholder Tips

Clip all loose threads and excess fabric from seams before turning. There is a lot of quilting,

which means a lot of little threads. These should be neat. Press each project. Add ribbon loops, curtain rings, or other interesting hooks. Be imaginative with the trim.

Making in Quantity

Do these assembly-line style. One person cuts all fabric patterns. The next person cuts all batting pieces. One person does all the pinning, and another sews. Someone takes out all pins and cuts off excess pieces of thread, trims seams, and adds loops, rings, etc. Someone irons everything.

Display Idea

The picnic basket seems like a good way to display these. Line the inside with red and white dish towel fabric, fill it with your wares, and off you go to the fair. Set up, open your basket, and you've got it in the bag. Display your best potholders on top. As they sell, bring out more and more. Toward the end of the day, when you're almost all sold out, close the basket and pile the remaining items on the lid.

Handkerchief Apron and Potholder

The butcher apron is made of handkerchief fabric and looks quite handsome on a man or woman. Don't scrimp on the size. It should wrap around even an ample body. Promote this as a barbecue apron, and make the matching potholder large enough to handle outdoor cooking.

The large plastic bracelet ring makes it easy to hang the potholder conveniently where it won't be misplaced, for example on your wrist!

This fabric is inexpensive, so use it lavishly. If you make potholders, make them oversized. The size and the fabric turn an ordinary item into something special.

Materials Needed

1 yard of fabric; red and white threads (if red plaid fabric is used as shown here) and needle; scissors; polyester batting 9 x 9 inches; 1 red plastic bracelet.

Directions

Use the pattern provided, and scale up to measure 12 inches across the top. Cut out one piece for the apron. Press under all edges ¼ inch, and stitch. The ties around the waist are 24 x 1½ inches wide after hemming. Around the neckband it is 24 x 1½ inches. Attach at each side, and press.

If you have enough fabric left from the yard (leaving two 10-inch squares for the potholder), sew on patch pockets as large as you like. If you use a border print or plaid fabric, be sure your pattern matches when you apply the pockets.

Potholder

Cut two squares 10 x 10 inches and one square of polyester batting 9 x 9 inches. Press a ½-inch hem in on all four sides of the 10-inch square. Place filler between the two squares of fabric, and topstitch together. Quilt by following the pattern of the fabric.

Catch bracelet at one corner with thread loops.

Variations

The preceding projects are variations of basic potholders in shapes of mitts, hearts, pan handles. Choose a color scheme, and overdo it.

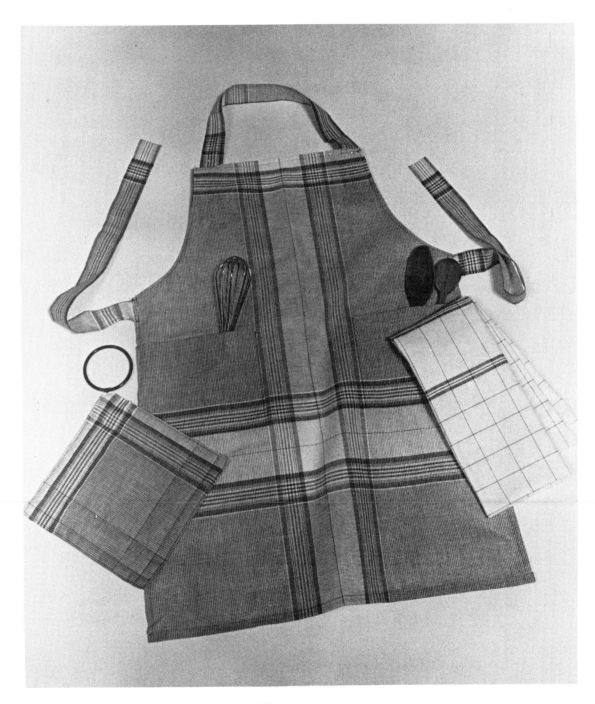

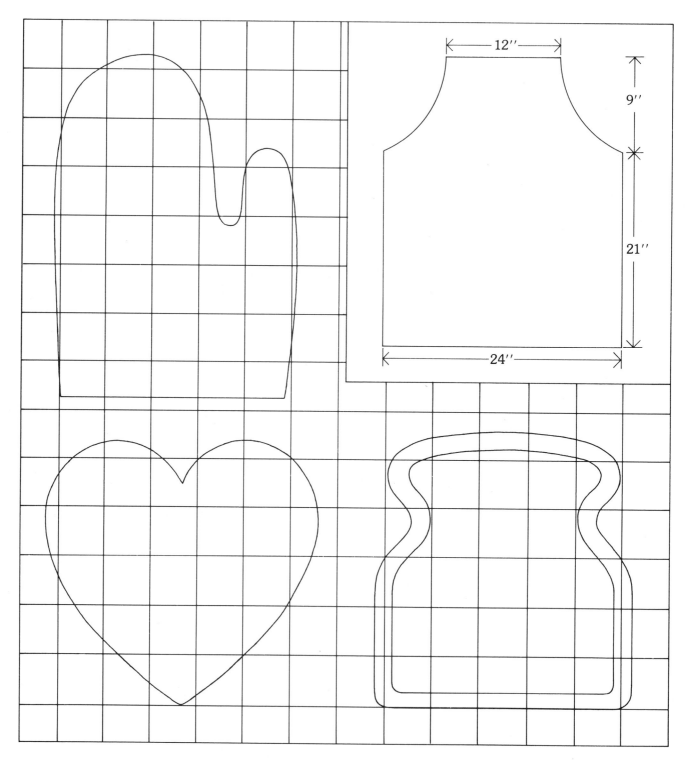

Embroidered Baby Pillowcase

There is nothing lovelier to make for a new baby than a hand-embroidered gift. The mother will treasure it always. I don't have a baby, nor do I know a new mother right now, but, when I got through with this project, I wished for one or the other so that I'd have an excuse to go on crafting. Baby projects are always satisfying to make. The colors and materials are so appealingly delicate, and the designs are fun to work on.

This is a perfect bazaar project because when one is finished, you will surely want to make more. These pillowcases can also be designed in regular sizes, and the embroidery can be applied to sheet hems as well.

I recommend simple designs for embroidery on linens and lingerie. Small pillowcases can be purchased, but it is an easy sewing project and much less expensive to make your own. Use the softest cotton you can find, and leave a generous hem at the opening. This will make the project luxurious.

Materials Needed

Cotton fabric or ready-made pillowcase; sharp embroidery needle and scissors; several different colors of floss; embroidery hoop; tracing paper; pencil; white eyelet trim; ½-inch-wide satin ribbon; needle and thread; 5-inch-wide cotton eyelet; pins; iron.

Directions

Trace and transfer design to the hem of the case. Begin by placing area to be worked in an embroidery hoop so that the fabric is held taut. Use three strands of floss for all stitches. Follow stitch key to work the embroidery. Do not secure threads with knots.

To press embroidery, pad your ironing board with bath towels. Place the embroidery right side down, and press with a steam iron. Do not permit the weight of the iron to rest on the embroidery. Go lightly over this area.

Next, cut eyelet trim so that it fits across hem of pillowcase. Cut enough ribbon to weave through the eyelet with enough left to make a bow in the center.

Pin 5-inch eyelet fabric to the top of the hem just above the embroidery. Place ribbon eyelet trim over the raw edge, and repin in position. Machine stitch to the case.

Make the bow, and pin it so that you can attach it with a whip or blind stitch. Press again, from the wrong side.

Variation

The inside of the hem can be lined with wide satin ribbon.

Making in Quantity

If you make one, you might purchase the pillowcase, but for quantity production it is practical to make your own.

Transfer all designs before you begin. Each person can then create his or her own needlework "painting." A small sewing project like this is easy to carry along with you. It fills wasted moments that we all experience in our daily routines.

Display Ideas

Keep it delicate. Keep it soft. Keep it pastel. Use baby carriers to display the pillows, or if the cases are folded, lay them on soft fabric or pastel tissue paper. Loosely tie pink, blue, and white satin ribbons around each. Tuck an artificial flower in each ribbon bow. Use baby props, such as a rattle, some talcum powder, a pretty jar of cotton balls. No bright, harshly colored toys. Sprinkle some powder on each case, and rub it in. Your booth will have the faint aroma of baby.

Party Place Mats

When making place mats, save the scraps for napkins. If there isn't enough material for full-size dinner napkins, make small cocktail sizes. The material used here matches Wall-Tex wallcovering, which gives you the opportunity to make projects from fabric and paper that match. Here I've covered berry baskets with the paper (see page 108), and even if you don't make complete sets for the bazaar, consider making one pretty setup like this for a display. Place it on one corner of your table where the rest of your projects can be viewed.

Materials Needed

1 yard of fabric (yields a place mat and napkin); needle and thread; scissors; ruler and pencil; iron.

Directions

Measure and cut two pieces of fabric 19 x 13 inches. Pin right sides together, and sew all but one short edge. Turn inside out, and press. Turn in raw edge, and stitch on the sewing machine. Stitch over all other edges as close as possible to outside. Press. Cut and hem fabric for napkins. Could any project be easier?

For the Christmas Booth

No bazaar is complete without a Christmas booth. Start early enough so you can have a variety of everyone's favorites. Tree ornaments are the most sought after as we all like to add some handmade goodies to the tree each year. Decorative candles, wreaths, centerpieces, candleholders, and hanging window decorations are a few of the things we all look for.

Stockings have gotten more and more elaborate every year. I have a friend who makes velvet stockings with big cuffs made from old pieces of lace.

Some are embroidered; others are covered with beads and sequins. All are embellished with lush plump satin or velvet bows. Felt is the standard material for Christmas crafting because it's so easy to work with. Create simple shapes, and use your imagination with the decorations.

Bread dough ornaments have become popular. A variation for the material is glue dough, which calls for a mixture of Elmer's Glue-All, cornstarch, and flour. The advantage is that no baking is involved.

Holiday Napkin Rings

Is there anyone who hasn't made napkin rings out of paper tubing? Certainly not a new idea, but so easy to update, perfect, and elaborate on that we can't overlook this project.

People think about setting a table for formal dining at the holidays. Try to imagine when you would use napkin rings, and design them with this in mind. Don't restrict yourself to Christmas and New Year's.

I once went to a Fourth of July picnic where the outdoor table was set with red, white, and blue ribboned napkin rings which held a red, white, or blue washcloth. "I use them all the time," I was told by the host. "The washcloths are cheaper than

paper, and I just toss them in the wash with everything else. No ironing."

However, the projects here are dressed up for winter holidays. They are romantically lacy, brightly beribboned, or adorned with pressed ferns. Make yours as lovely as possible.

Materials Needed

Enough paper tubing (from paper towels, toilet tissue, etc.) to make several 1½-inch rings; pencil; craft knife or razor blade; decorations, such as pressed flowers and ferns, buttons, lace, ribbons, doilies, decals; glue; Krylon clear spray varnish; spray or acrylic paint; paint brush; scissors; black felt-tip marker.

Directions

Use paper tubing to make as many 1½-inch napkin rings as you need. If you are selling them, make up sets of four or six that match or contrast in an appealing way.

Mark off and cut each ring from the tube. The more accurate the cuts, the better the finished project. If the design is to be lacy and romantic, use white or pale pink paint. Spray paint or brush acrylic paint on each one. If you cover the rings with wrapping paper or fabric, painting is unnecessary.

Select ribbons, lace, or paper doilies to cover or edge each one. Place a decal, such as the butterfly or roses shown here, in the center of each. You can also cut out your own designs from wrapping paper, cards, etc. The butterfly antennae are drawn on with a marker.

Spray varnish each one so that it is sealed, shiny, and sturdy. The inside should be finished with paint, paper, or ribbon so that it looks complete.

Variations

The fern-covered rings are very pretty on a holiday table. You can also use pressed flowers chosen for the occasion. Buttercups press well and retain their color. For these you will have to start early. The ferns came from a florist and took approximately a week to press. Leave this much time for most natural material.

Spray the ferns with Krylon clear spray varnish to keep them from shedding when they are being glued to the white background. Spread glue generously on the napkin ring, and set the fern gently down. Pat with a slightly damp sponge. Cut the excess from the edges if it is larger than the ring. Let this dry, and spray with several coats of varnish.

One of the other rings is covered with paper, left over from the berry basket. You can make a set to match a basket that you've covered. The Christmas ring is made from red-and-white checked ribbon with a "Merry Christmas" paper seal attached.

Making in Quantity

Working in a team is the best way to make these, unless you work on them now and then, in your spare time. I found it tiring to make the same thing over and over and then to begin again with a new design. When people work together, everyone can design a set. At the end of one gathering you will have a nice variety of designs for all occasions. This is a good time to get out the scraps, remnants, odds and ends from the sewing box.

Display Ideas

These should be displayed as they would be used. Make your setup as elegant or gay as pos-

sible. We know they're toilet-paper tubes, the buyers probably know they're toilet-paper tubes, but if you do everything possible to detract from this fact, it may never enter their minds.

The napkins used here are pieces of remnant fabric. Select colors that make your project look the best. "Set" a card table with a beautiful lacy tablecloth or a white embroidered old-fashioned covering. Avoid prints or checks that would detract from the napkin rings. Have an arrangement of greens or a few plants on the table. Create an environment to show how they can best be used.

Another way to display them is in gift boxes from the five-and-dime. They should be the right size to hold sets of four or six, whichever you decide on. Fill the box with colorful tissue; place each napkin ring in the box, with the design showing. Crinkle the tissue around the rings so they are nestled in the box. This will make it very enticing to purchase for immediate gift giving. Note: When figuring cost, don't forget to include the box in your charge. In addition, consider tying each with a satin ribbon.

Cross-Stitch Napkins

The napkin with the Christmas tree design in the corner is done in cross-stitch. This is a good design for embroidery because it is small and requires a minimum of time. You can buy inexpensive napkins to decorate or make your own. Sell a set of them with the Christmas napkin rings for an elegant boxed gift. If you feel ambitious, make place mats to match.

Materials Needed

Tracing paper; pencil; 6-strand embroidery floss; pieces of washable cotton; sharp embroidery needle; scissors.

Directions

Make cotton luncheon napkins 16 inches square, and scallop the edges. Finish them off with embroidery floss in the same or contrasting color. White on white is nice. If you're making a set for yourself, choose colors to match your china or tablecloth.

Trace and transfer design to fabric. Determine your colors for each design. Make all underneath threads in one direction and all top threads in the opposite direction. Keep the stitches as even as possible with the ends of the crosses touching.

Start from the underside of the material. Do not knot the thread. Leave it loose, and don't pull stitches too tightly. Start and finish all ends by running them under previous stitches on the wrong side.

Christmas Projects That Last All Year

When you open all those presents on Christmas morning, save the wrapping paper, cards, ribbons, and tags. Everything can be recycled for other projects throughout the book. These two ideas can be made with the wrappings. Frames and small boxes are very popular bazaar items.

The frame is the inexpensive dime-store variety. When wrapped with paper and varnished, it becomes instantly interesting. Make a number of them with all different papers. Remove the glass from the frame. Cut strips of paper to size and glue to the frame. Press down and carefully smooth the paper over the frame. Let dry. Reassemble frames. Do all spray varnishing at once.

The holly trinket box is painted with red acrylic paint. Cut a band of Christmas paper, and glue around the bottom. Cut out a sprig of paper holly, and glue to the top. Spray three or four coats of clear varnish over the inside and outside. Because the paper is thin, you'll be able to coat it quickly, making it a good project for a Christmas booth.

Wine Gift Wrap

This is a good bazaar item because it's a project that anyone can make. It is also a good way to wrap a bottle of wine to give as a last-minute gift. To make these for a seasonal bazaar, stencil <u>Cheers</u> or <u>Merry Christmas</u> across each finished bag. It's easy to do this with acrylic paint.

Use a linen napkin or a dish towel (or any firm fabric such as muslin), and cut to 12 x 14½ inches. Turn under along one 12-inch side for top hem. If you use a napkin or dish towel, you won't need a hem. The edges will already be finished.

Fold in half lengthwise so you have a doubled piece 6 x 14 inches with the right sides together.

Hem along the 14-inch wrong side and across the bottom. Turn to the right side.

Slip a bottle of wine into the bag, and tie with a fat piece of yarn or ribbon in a matching color. At Christmastime use a red and white boldly striped napkin. The cost will be under $2. Linen napkins come in all colors. Pick the one that expresses the occasion best.

Display Ideas

Display one or two filled with a bottle. Add gift cards tied to the yarn.

Coordinated Christmas Food Booth

Have the kids help with this rainy-day project. Save up all those empty coffee, mayonnaise, and jelly jars, aluminum-foil loaf pans, plastic plant pots, and inexpensive juice glasses.

One of the nicest ways to arrange a food booth is with a coordinated color or theme. Keep it simple, emphasizing the appeal of the food.

Create the patterns at random with dots of red and white acrylic paint applied with an artist's brush. No painting talent is required. Just put dots on everything. Put red dots inside white dots. Make shapes of dots. Write words in free hand with a brush and paint.

Cover the tops with doilies, red and white fabric, paper, or lace. Tie red and white satin ribbon around loaves of bread. Wrap bottle necks with red and white polka-dot seam binding. Think red and white dots, and you'll even be making everything with cranberries.

Petal Wrap for Food Jars

Use scraps of calico, satin, cotton prints to make a delightful food jar wrap that is quick and easy.

Measure one side and bottom of a jar. Double these measurements. For example, if the jar is 5 inches high and 3 inches across the bottom, cut a 16-inch diameter circle of fabric. Fold the circle in half, in half again, and in half again. Cut the edge into a petal about 2 inches deep. Unfold.

Place the jar in the center of the circle, and gather the edges up around the neck of the jar. Tie with cord or ribbon or embroidery thread. Cut a circle of colored paper or a doily the size of the lid. Glue it to the top. Make a label (red-border mailing or self-sticking), and adhere it to the front of the wrap.

Variations

Make a batch of these in different colors of gingham, and tie with contrasting ribbons for a co-ordinated food booth. Paint matching gingham pattern on food tins.

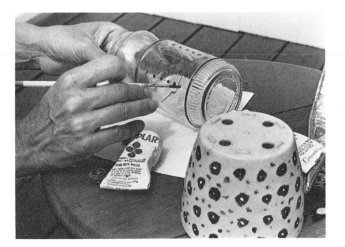

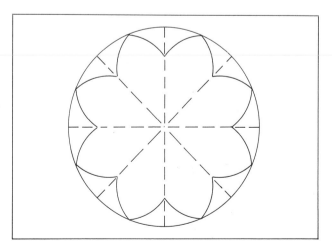

Stained Glass Window Ornaments

These ornaments aren't really done in the true stained glass technique, but they are inspired by this craft. The glass hanging-decorations are much easier to make with simple materials you may have around the house.

Materials Needed

2 pieces of 4-x-4-inch thin glass (can be cut at hardware store); food coloring; Elmer's Glue-All; paintbrush; Mystik tape ½ inch wide; tracing paper; nylon filament (hardware store); felt marker; pencil.

Directions

Glue paint is made by adding food coloring to white glue. It will adhere to almost any surface, including glass. All designs shown here will fit on a 4-x-4-inch square. Trace a design on paper, and tape it to your work surface. Tape the glass square over the design.

Mix colors to be used in small cups. Paint the colors on. Be sure to keep side-by-side colors separate. Let each color dry before adding another. The details can be drawn on with a felt marker.

When the colors are dry, place the second square over the design to protect it. Use Mystik tape to bind the edges. Trim at the corners for a neat finish.

Hang the decoration by a loop made from fine nylon filament.

Making in Quantity

If you are making these in quantity, food colors can be added individually to a number of 1¼-ounce glue containers, creating a selection of ready-made glue paint containers.

Variation

Designs of multicolored dots can be made easily by using the glue container as an applicator. Just squeeze each dot where you want it.

Display Ideas

It would be best if these could be displayed in a window, but this is probably inappropriate at a bazaar. Do the best you can to hang them so light shines through. Create a display tree of branches. Spray them silver, and arrange in a bucket of sand. Cover sand and bucket with felt skirt.

Clothespin Wreath

Wreaths made from all kinds of material are always popular during the Christmas season. I have made many of them from natural material and in my book *Wildcrafts* included a section of some of the more unusual. These were made from spices, dried flowers, and shells. But this clothespin wreath is quite different.

Made from two types of clothespins, it is sprinkled with red "glue" berries, and it is quite easy to make one or several. This is one of those projects made from ordinary materials that, while recognizable, are appreciated for their cleverness.

Materials Needed

A piece of stiff corrugated cardboard or Fome Cor (art supply store) 10 x 10 inches; 1 package of regular wooden clothespins, 1 package of spring-type wooden clothespins; Elmer's Glue-All; corn-

starch; flour; 1 can of Krylon green enamel spray paint; red food coloring or acrylic paint; 1½-inch-wide red ribbon for bow.

Directions

To make the base for the clothespin wreath, cut a 10-x-10-inch circle out of stiff corrugated cardboard or Fome Cor.

Next, cut a 5-inch-diameter hole in the center. The 2½-inch-wide disk you have created will hold the clothespins. Spray paint all the clothespins green. An easy way to do this is on a clothesline.

Put one regular clothespin on the disk. Place a spring-type pin next to it, and alternate in this manner until the disk is full. Make another layer by gluing more regular clothespins on top of the first layer, but put them on top of the regular pins only, not on top of the spring-type pins. When doing this, reverse the position so that the top layer lies head to toe on the bottom layer.

The red cranberries are formed from glue dough. Mix together ¼ cup each of Elmer's Glue-All, cornstarch, and flour in a bowl. Roll into cranberry-size balls. If the mixture seems too dry, add glue. If too wet, add flour and cornstarch. Let the balls dry for twenty-four hours.

When the balls are dry, paint each with red acrylic paint, or glue paint, to save money. This is done by mixing red food coloring with Elmer's glue and brushing it over the balls. Place them here and there on wreath. Leave to dry.

Make a pretty bow of grosgrain ribbon, and glue or attach with thread to the bottom of the wreath. Tie a piece of string or cord to the back of one of the clothespins for easy hanging.

Variations

Add real holly or dried flowers here and there on the clothespins. Make several smaller wreaths. Make an 8-inch-diameter hanging window decoration by fixing clothespins around a 5-inch-diameter disk.

Making in Quantity

The only timesaving device I can think of for making these in quantity is to use red beads for the cranberries, but the glue dough method saves money.

If you can find disks that are precut, this will be an added time-saver. However, they must be made of cardboard or Fome Cor so that the clothespins will fit on it. Plastic foam is too thick.

Display Ideas

These wreaths are heavy, so if hung, they must be placed on a sturdy background. A panel of barnsiding is interesting-looking and can be purchased in a panel or lumber store. It's easy to glue to a piece of plywood or tack to a wall where the booth is set up.

Crocheted Christmas Angel

This project was sent to me by Sally George, who owns The Crochet Works in Baker, Oregon. Her original designs and patterns are sold, through her mail-order catalog, all over the country, and she can tell us a lot about what people are buying and selling at bazaars.

The projects that she has shared with us are easy enough for a beginner to make, according to her customers, who say that the instructions can be followed by an inexperienced crocheter. One of the women who order from her writes, "My daughter and I have made 500 angels and still have orders to fill. We need a new pattern, having worn out the original."

While the instructions may seem long, they are not difficult. "This project is a little different from the usual trees and stockings, which also sell well," Sally says. "But of course I do have wreaths, flat trees, mice, stockings, and bells for those who want them."

The following is reprinted with the permission of Sally George of The Crocket Works. (See Source List of Materials to order catalog of designs.)

Materials Needed

4-ply knitting worsted weight yarn, a few ounces each of pale pink for heads and arms, yellow for halos and wings, browns and yellows for hair, white for trim, and any color you desire for the dresses. You'll need some blue or brown yarn for eyes and a bit of red embroidery floss for the mouth, Dacron batting, and a yarn needle. Hooks: G gauge: 4 sc = 1 inch, 4½ sc rows = 1 inch

Directions

Head

Starting at top, with pink and G hook, ch 2.
Rnd 1: 6 sc in 2nd ch from hook, do not join, but mark rounds with yarn of contrasting color.
Rnd 2: 2 sc in ea sc around (12 sc).
Rnd 3: (1 sc in next sc, 2 sc in next sc) 6 times (18 sc).
Next 3 rnds: sc in eac sc. Begin stuffing with Dacron batting.
Rnd 7: (1 sc in next sc, 1 dec in next 2 sc) 6 times (12 sc).
Rnd 8: (dec in next 2 sc) 6 times, sl st to next sc, end off.

Arms: Make 2

With pink and G hook, ch 8. Sc in 2nd ch from hook and ea of next 5 ch, 3 sc in end ch; working along other side of ch, sc in ea ch, end off, leaving 6 inches of yarn for sewing. Fold piece in half lengthwise, and sew sides together with overcast sts, catching the outside lps. By pulling the sts slightly, you can make the arm curve. For bendable arms, put a pipe cleaner in before sewing.

Halo

With yellow and G hook, ch 25 tightly (or 5 inches), join, leaving 3 inches to sew with.

Wings: Make 2

With yellow and G hook, ch 13.
Row 1: sl st in 2nd ch from hook, sc in ea of next 3 ch, 2 sc in next ch, sc in next ch, dc in next ch, ch 1, holding back last lp of ea st, dc in ea of next 4 ch (5 lps on hook), yo and through all 5 lps for cluster, dc in last ch, ch 1, turn.
Row 2: sc in dc, sc in top of cluster, sk ch, sc in

dc, sc in next sc, 2 sc, sl st in next sc, ch 1, turn.

Row 3: sk sl st, sl st in sc, sc in next sc, 2 sc in next sc, sc in ea of next 3 sc, 2 sc in next sc, 2 sc in last sc, 2 sc in first part of pc st of dc, sl st in next part of dc pc st, join to beginning ch, end off, leaving 3 inches of yarn for sewing.

Dress

Note, When working rnds in sc that are joined with a sl st, I always work the first sc into the same sc that is sl st'd into or the joining st. That way, at the end of ea rnd, all the sl sts line up on top of ea other and are not counted nor worked into.

Use color of choice and G hook, starting at top, ch 8, join to form ring, ch 1.

Rnd 1: sc in ea ch, join, ch 1 (8 sc).

Rnd 2: sc in ea sc around, join, ch 1.

Rnd 3: sc in first 2 sc, 2 sc in next sc, sc in ea of next 3 sc, 2 sc in next sc, sc in last sc, join, ch 1 (10 sc).

Rnd 4: sc in first 2 sc, 2 sc in next sc, sc in ea of next 4 sc, 2 sc in next sc, sc in last 2 sc, join, ch 1 (12 sc).

Rnd 5: sc in first 3 sc, 2 sc in next sc, sc in ea of next 4 sc, 2 sc in next sc, sc in last 3 sc, join, ch 1 (14 sc).

Rnd 6: 2 sc in first sc, sc in rest of sc around, join (15 sc).

Rnd 7: (ch 4, sk 1 sc, sl st in next sc) 7 times, ch 2, dc in joining st (8 lps).

Next 3 rnds: (ch 5, sl st in next lp) 7 times, ch 3, dc in dc that joined previous rnd.

Rnd 11: 3 dc in same dc just worked into, sl st in next lp making shell (ch 5, sl st in next lp, 3 dc in sl st between next 2 lps, sl st in next lp) 3 times, ch 3, dc in 1st dc of shell (4 lps and 4 shells).

Rnd 12: (ch 5, sl st in top of shell, ch 5, sl st in next lp) 3 times, ch 5, sl st into shell, ch 3, dc in dc of previous rnd (8 lps).

Rnd 13: (ch 1, dc) 3 times in same dc just worked into, ch 1, sl st in next lp, * (ch 1, dc) 3 times in sl st between next 2 lps, ch 1, sl st to next lp, repeat from * around, join to 1st shell, end off.

Sleeve

ch 2 with same yarn and hook.

Rnd 1: 6 sc in 2nd ch from hook, join, ch 1 (6 sc).

Next 2 rnds: sc in ea sc around, join, ch 1.

Rnd 4: (sc in next 2 sc, 2 sc in next sc) twice, join, ch 1 (8 sc).

Rnd 5: (sc in ea of next 3 sc, 2 sc in next sc) twice, join (10 sc).

Rnd 6: ch 4, sk joining st and next sc, sl st in next sc (ch 4, sk next sc, sl st in next sc) 3 times, ch 2, dc sl st.

Rnd 7: (ch 5, sl st in next lp) 4 times, ch 3, dc in dc joining previous rnd.

Rnd 8: * (ch 1, dc) twice in st between lps, ch 1, sl st to next lp, repeat from * *only once,* making 2 shells, ch 3, turn.

Rnd 9: sk ch 1, sl st in next dc (ch 1, dc) twice in sl st between shells, ch 3, sl st in 3rd from hook for picot (dc, ch 1) twice in same st as dc's made before picot, sl st to center dc in next shell, ch 3, sl st in next dc (ch 3, sl st in lp, ch 3, sl st in sl st) 3 times, ch 3, sl st in lp, end off.

Finishing

With dress yarn, sew head to neck of dress. Place arms in sleeves so hands show at edge. Sew in place with dress yarn. Sew sleeve at "shoulders" of dress, taking sts in top 3 rnds of dress. With yellow, sew on wings. Pull down on her skirt on one side to make her "fly."

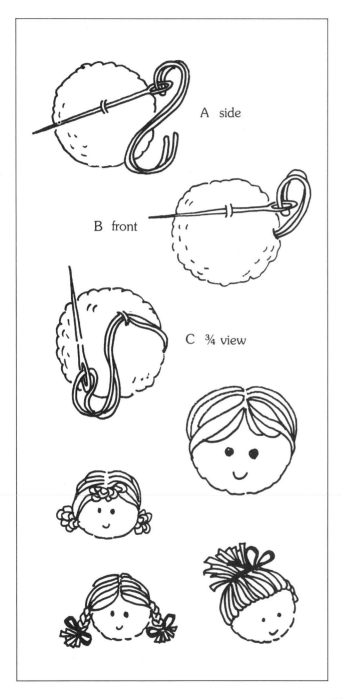

A side

B front

C ¾ view

Add hair with yarn, and place halo on top of hair with sl st at the back; tack only in that place so the halo will float over the head. Embroider features on face. Make a hanging loop out of sewing thread, and attach to top of head.

Embroidering the Faces

Keep it simple. Use French knots in yarn for eyes, or sew on a small sequin. Use stem stitch with floss for mouth (will only take 3 or 4 stitches), or glue on half sequin. Sally doesn't bother with a mouth. She finds it clumsy.

Hairstyles

Thread yarn needle so strand yarn is doubled. Take long stitches from one side of head (A) to other side (C), going under an sc loop at top center of head (B) (where the part would be). Continue in this manner until entire head is covered.

Crochet Abbreviations

beg—begin, beginning; bet—between; bl—block; cc—contrasting color; ch—chain; cl—cluster; dc—double crochet; dec—decrease; dtr—double treble crochet; gm—gram; hdc—half double crochet; in(s) or —inch(es); inc—increase; incl—including; lp—loop; oz9s0—ounce9s0; pat—pattern; pc—picot; rem—remaining; rnd(s)—round; rpt—repeat; sc—single crochet; sk—skip; skn—skein; sl—slip; sl st—slip stitch; sp—space; st(s)—stitch(es); thru—through; tog—together; tr—triple crochet; work even—work without in or dec; yd(s)—yard(s); yo—yarn over hook; *—repeat whatever follows the * as many times as specified; ()—do what is in parentheses.

Snowflake Tree Ornament

The crochet snowflake is another Sally George design. Her customers make lots and lots of these each year. This and the angel (her favorite) are the two best bazaar sellers as reported by her customers. The snowflake pattern provided here is one of ten that she has available.

Materials Needed

#6 steel hook, Knit-Cro Sheen

Directions

Snowflake approximately 4½ inches across

Ch 4, join with sl st to form ring, ch 3.

Rnd 1: 11 dc into ring, join at top of ch 3.

Rnd 2: ch 3, 2 dc in same st, ch 2, sk 1 dc, * 3 dc in next dc, ch 2, sk 1 dc, repeat from * around, join.

Rnd 3: ch 3, 1 dc in same st, 3 dc in next dc, 2 dc in next dc, * 2 dc in next dc, 3 dc in next dc, 2 dc, in next dc, repeat from * around, join.

Rnd 4: * ch 3, sl st in same st, ch 7, sl st in 4th ch from hook, dc in ea of next 5 dc, holding the last loops of ea dc on the hook until there are 6 loops on hook, yo and thru all 6 loops (ch 5, sl st in 4th ch from hook for picot) 4 times, sl st into base of 3rd picot from hook, ch 5, sl st in 4th ch from hook, sl st into base of next picot, ch 5, sl st in 4th ch from hook, sl st into top of cluster of dcs, ch 3, sl st into next dc, ch 3, sl st in same st, ch 5, sl st into 4th ch from hook, ch 1, sl st into next dc, repeat from * around, join, end off.

Display Ideas

Fill a small tree with snowflakes. They will look beautiful against the green branches. Use this as a display, but have boxed sets of four or six for selling. Look for white jewelry boxes in the five-and-ten. Take the finished project with you when buying the size you need. Cover the table with a lacy or crocheted cloth, preferably white. This will create a winter feeling (even in July) that's in keeping with the delicate snowflakes.

Have red and green ½-inch satin ribbons cut to exact lengths for tying around each box as it is sold. Consider adding gift tags or a Christmas seal to the box.

Fido's Bone

Don't forget the family pet when creating projects. Everyone will want at least one pet ornament on the tree at Christmas. The designs provided here can be cut from felt. They are easy to stitch up, fill with biscuits, and hang. This is an inexpensive no-work item. Another good quick craft.

Materials Needed

1 piece of red felt 9 x 10 inches; ribbon or felt loop 6 inches x ½ inch; small piece of green felt; needle and thread.

Directions

Fold the red felt in half so it is 9 x 5 inches. Trace pattern of the bone, scale it up, pin it to felt, and cut it out. Stitch all around, leaving an opening at the top large enough to fill "bone" with puppy biscuits. Sew ribbon loop to the top. Cut tiny bone decoration from green felt, and glue it in place.

Display Ideas

Hang these from a pegboard or on branches that are secured in a sand-filled bucket.

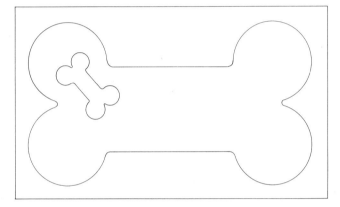

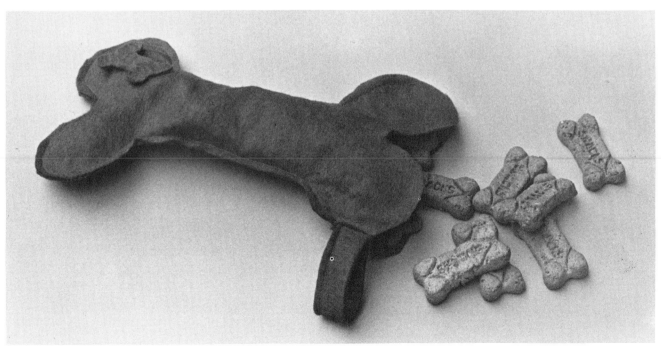

There are many containers, jars, boxes, and wrappings that we consider throwaways. If we begin to look at all outer packaging as potential projects, it's amazing how much we can recycle. We've all been exposed to the kind of recycled projects that are so obvious we know exactly what they were made from. Would you pay for something that is made from a detergent box if you could make it yourself? When using scrap material as the basis for your projects, you will have to make up in imagination, design, and crafting technique what you save in money. The first trick is to forget that it is a throwaway item. The next trick is to conceal it so nobody else will recognize what it is.

Once you start crafting, your scraps become treasures. It is from these little salvaged pieces of material that many interesting and inexpensive projects are created. Select scraps that combine well together in color and pattern for the pincushions shown on page 113. Save the more delicate fabrics and patterns for sachets. Since these projects are small, you can afford the extra time to pay attention to details.

The two scissor and needle holders on page 128 were made from the leftover potholder material (page 107), and the potholder was made from apron scraps. The eyeglass cases on page 124 were made from scraps left over from the tote bag projects on page 73. Scraps of satin from the appliqués on page 73 cover a plastic plant pot to hold baked goods on page 29. The following are some of the ways to use those throwaways for easy and profitable projects. Use your imagination to design your own projects from the things you have left over.

Pretty Scrap Potholder

Potholders can be made in the same way as the strip pincushions except that you will need larger pieces and can eliminate the stuffing. Remnants of lace, ribbons, or binding are used to finish off the edges. The more delicate the fabric, the more the holder will look like a gift, and a useful one at that.

Materials Needed

9 strips of 6-inch-long fabric; 3 layers of 6-inch-square cotton or polyester batting; 1 layer of 6-inch-square piece of fabric for the back (or 9 more 6-inch-long strips); needle and thread; scissors; iron.

Directions

As with the pincushion, place ¾- to 1½-inch strips side by side to arrange a pleasing placement of colors and patterns. Sew these together, right sides facing. Press seams in one direction. Do this for the front and back of the potholder, or use a solid fabric for the back. Sew with right sides together, leaving enough of an opening to turn right side out. Insert three layers of batting. Turn open end in and hand stitch closed.

Variations

Stitch the front and back together with the right sides facing out. Cover the raw edges with binding or lace or ribbon. Attach ring or ribbon loop in one corner for hanging.

Making in Quantity

See pincushion directions for making these in quantity. Quantities of lace are available at wholesale prices (see Source List).

Display Ideas

Unless you are making many potholders in beautiful, unusual fabrics, it is best to combine this item with other kitchen projects. Make solid butcher's aprons, for example, and attach bright scrap potholders with Velcro. Or use this scrap idea to make pockets for the aprons. Cover oatmeal containers with the matching scraps, and spray with Scotchgard fabric protector. These can be used to hold wooden spoons and spatulas or as canisters. With very little effort and no money you will have an outstanding display.

Berry Baskets

Paper berry baskets from the supermarket can be turned into handsome containers for more uses than you can think of. They can also be waterproofed for holding plants. They come in at least three or four sizes so they lend themselves to small and larger items to fit on a windowsill, for use as a centerpiece or on a desk. When lined up on a shelf, they create an attractive way to hold odds and ends within easy reach.

According to the basic rule that says, When you make something from a throwaway, it shouldn't be obvious that it's a throwaway, a berry basket is easy to disguise. The easiest way to do this is with a cover-up. Paper or fabric can effectively turn a plain throwaway into a pretty object.

If you are using fabric, choose it carefully. Since only a very small amount is needed, pick an elegant design that will elevate the object to centerpiece status. Add a beautiful ribbon, and fill it with dried flowers or wrapped candies.

The projects here are covered with paper. Some use greeting or wrapping papers; others are covered with Wall-Tex vinyl wall covering. The variety of patterns is endless, and you can choose themes

according to what each will hold. A baby design for the nursery holds cotton balls, for example. Rickrack trim is used for a sewing container. Floral prints are used to hold a bouquet of dried flowers. The paper-covered baskets have an added dimension that makes them appear less ordinary than plain containers.

Materials Needed

Berry basket; wrapping paper or wallcovering or fabric; Elmer's Glue-All; sponge; scissors; pencil; can of Krylon clear spray varnish.

Directions

Place the basket on the paper. Trace around one side and the bottom. Cut these pieces out. Use them to trace and cut a piece for each side, inside and out, as well as the inside bottom. This is easier than measuring, as each basket is slightly different and the shapes are not perfectly regular. Cut each piece slightly larger than the actual dimension to allow for overlap at the edges. If your paper has a pattern that must be matched, allow for this when cutting, and plan accordingly.

Spread glue over each piece, and apply it to the

basket. The bottom of the inside and underside should be glued last. Wipe away any excess glue with a sponge. Let this dry for at least a half hour. The material of the basket is very absorbent and should have time to dry thoroughly.

Spray the finished basket with clear Krylon varnish. Be sure to coat all sides, inside and out. This will take minutes to dry and should be repeated three or four times.

The varnish gives the basket a high gloss. It will be sturdy, waterproof, and chinalike in appearance. Suddenly a scrap material has some glamour.

Variations

If you are covering these with fabric, printed polished cotton works well. Satin and velvet will change the appearance considerably. It is more difficult to work with fabric because it frays and you must be careful not to get any glue on the surface. If you use a thick fabric, such as velvet, the edges must be cut carefully to butt against one another. When using cotton, spray the surface with Scotchgard fabric protector.

To apply fabric, cut each piece correctly. Spray the back of the fabric with an adhesive, such as 3M brand Spra-Ment for easy application.

Making in Quantity

When working on several baskets, order a roll of wallpaper in each of the different designs you select. This is much less expensive than using wrapping paper. You will have less variety, but you will get more paper for your money.

However, if you select paper with matching fabric, such as the Wall-Tex collection, you can make matching items from the fabric. Napkins and place mats are ideal for this purpose.

Work on baskets of one size all at once. Trace the side and bottom of one, and make a template from heavier paper (such as shirtboard) for cutting out as many pieces as needed.

Dilute Elmer's glue with a few drops of water in a shallow dish. Use a sponge brush applicator (hardware store) to spread glue over each piece of paper as needed.

Complete all the baskets at one time. Then spray varnish at one time. If you are working in a group, one person cuts the paper, two or three can be gluing them onto the baskets, and the first person is then free to spray each as it is ready. By the time you finish spraying the last basket the first will be dry, and you can reapply a coat to each one. The project is great fun as a group activity. If the kids want to help, have them trace templates or cut out pieces.

Display Ideas

If you can put up shelves (see Booth Displays), line the baskets along them, varying the sizes, colors, and patterns. Fill a few of them with interesting objects. When displaying them on a table, select a few that suggest their uses and fill them. One might hold a plant; another, sewing notions; another, food. Stack the rest of them in an interesting way.

These baskets are especially nice as planters and food containers. Make them to use at either of these booths.

Paint Bucket Planters

This isn't a throwaway item unless you've used it first while painting a large area. A paper bucket found in most hardware and paint stores comes in two sizes. Both sell for approximately 50 cents and are quite versatile. Some are plain white, best for our purposes. Others have printing on them and must be spray painted or covered with paper or fabric. Painting is the easiest, and the technique used here is simple decoupage. These buckets can be used for catchalls in the bathroom or to organize small toys in a child's room. They are perfect for cooking utensils as well as for holding tennis balls. Large balls of yarn are easily stored in them, too.

Materials Needed

Paper paint bucket; acrylic or spray paint, brush (if using acrylic paint); white glue; scissors; sponge; wrapping paper with large designs; Krylon clear spray varnish.

Directions

Paint the bucket a bright color. If you are making one project, it is economical to use acrylic paint, which comes in small tubes. If you are making several, spray paint is easy—and economical if several are sprayed in one color. The inside can be a contrasting color or the same as the outside.

Select wrapping paper that is colorful and bold so that its design will look good on the buckets. Cut away surrounding white paper, and glue each design to the bucket. Pat down with damp sponge, and wipe away excess glue. Let this dry. Spray a coating of varnish over all exposed surfaces.

Variations

It takes time to cut out the paper designs. To speed up the decoration process, use decals, which

come in a variety of designs and sizes. Meyercord is the manufacturer of the largest variety, and a display can be found in most five-and-ten-cent stores. Craft shops often sell rub-on transfers for decoupage.

Fabric and paper coverings are not easy to apply. The bucket shapes make it difficult to apply the paper or fabric without wrinkles, folds, and creases.

Making in Quantity

If you are making these to sell as plant holders or for food containers, the only easy and economical way is to spray paint them. One person can do this ahead of time. In this way a group can then concentrate on cutting out and applying all the designs. Suggest that everyone save wrapping paper from gifts received throughout the year.

Display Ideas

These buckets practically display themselves. If they are brightly painted and the decorations are bold, they will attract attention any way you display them. Use them at the plant or food booths. If it is a Christmas bazaar, use Christmas wrapping paper designs, and fill each with holly or a Christmas cactus plant. Cover your display area with bright tissue, a red tablecloth, green fabric, or a paper holiday tablecloth.

Place each bucket on a colored plastic-coated paper plate. Surround each with tiny Christmas balls, greens, or similar ornaments.

Fabric lunch bags p. 49

Flower arrangement p. 154

Decorative soaps p. 42

Embroidered baby pillowcase p. 85

Ankle art p. 37

Baby T's p. 44

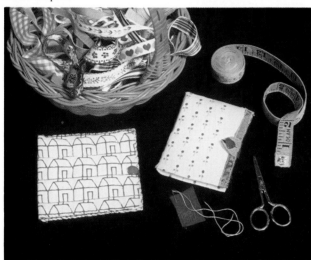

Sewing aids p. 128

Scrap-strip pincushions p. 113

Pressed rose box p. 50

Fantasy finish frames p. 166

Note pad bindings p. 71

Miniature picture plaques p. 160

Coordinated Christmas food booth p. 94

Satin evening bags p. 78

Cross-stitch napkins p. 90

Cosmetic bow box p. 64

Tissue covers p. 141

Sachets p. 115

Soap holder and towels p. 47

Party placemat p. 87

Berry baskets p. 108

Berry baskets p. 108

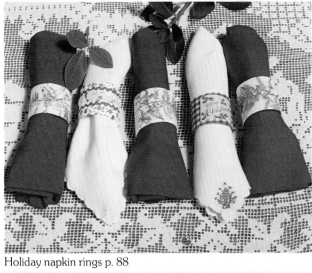

Holiday napkin rings p. 88

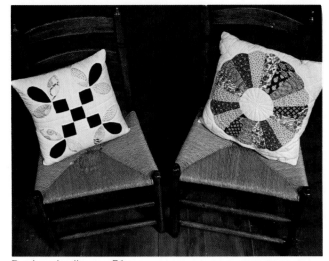

Patchwork pillows p. 76

Cricket stool p. 57

Porcelain flower frame p. 164

Letter box p. 65

Decoupage trinket boxes p. 55

Velvet tote bags p. 73

Party placemat p. 87

Paper patchwork box p. 168

Bottles that blossom p. 138

Quilted potholders p. 80

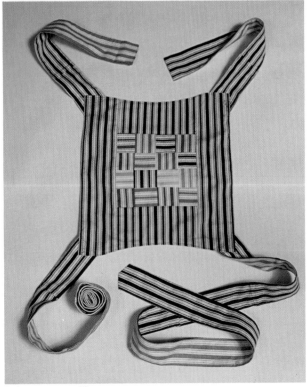

Baby carrier p. 62

Paint bucket planters p. 111

Scrap Strip Pincushion

This pincushion is 4 inches square. Use your imagination when selecting materials that go together in color and design. Choose pastel colors and small printed fabric for a delicate, light cushion. Or use a combination of dark velvets for a completely different style. You can use this same technique to make smaller sachets and ornaments, or increase the size for throw pillows. Strips of scraps can even be the basis for a baby carriage coverlet.

Materials Needed

Strips of fabric scraps 6 inches long and from ¾ to 1¼ inches wide (9 strips for one side of a 6-inch pincushion; the back can be solid or made of fabric strips also); needle and thread; scissors; stuffing material (cotton batting or polyester batting, old nylon stockings, birdseed).

Directions

Arrange the nine strips side by side, making sure that each one goes well with the one next to it. With right sides facing, sew the strips together lengthwise until you have a 6-inch square. Press all seams so they go in one direction.

Create a square or diagonal design. For a diagonal design cut the square of strips as indicated in the drawing. Either make another square for the back, or use one piece of fabric cut to 4½ x 4½ inches square.

Pin the right sides of fabric together, and stitch around three and a half sides, leaving a ¼-inch seam. Turn to the right side. Stuff the pincushion with one of the recommended fillers. Make sure you get into all corners. Hand stitch the closing.

Variations

Whenever an interesting project calls for scrap material and very little time and effort, it is rewarding. And when you can use the scraps from the scrap project, it is even more satisfying. The smaller pincushion (or ornament or sachet) is made from the material cut from the corners of the larger pincushion. Sew these together, matching strips. You will have two squares that look like the drawing. With right sides facing, sew together. Leave enough of an opening to turn right side out. Stuff, and sew opening by hand. Attach a loop of ribbon or yarn for hanging.

Making in Quantity

If all the pincushions are made the same size, it is easier than making each one different. However, if you have little pieces of odd scraps, it makes more sense to use them in the best way you can.

Cut all strips for all cushions at one time. While one person does all the running up of seams on the sewing machine, another can be pressing and preparing them for the final sewing step. Someone else can stuff and stitch all closings by hand.

If you work on these in your spare time, while watching television, for example, the work will be done quickly even when you sew all of them by hand.

Display Ideas

Create an interesting basket of colorful threads and ribbons. Add a thimble and scissors, possibly a tape measure. Stick pins into a pincushion or two, and arrange a group of them in the basket. Consider lining the basket with a solid fabric, old lace, or pretty paper. When my mother makes these, she cuts up used greeting cards to make small gift card enclosures. Punch a hole in one corner for a ribbon, and cut the edges straight or with pinking shears. Attach to the corner of each pincushion.

For Christmas ornament display, hang several from branches that are held in a bucket of sand or florist clay or in a block of plastic foam.

Sachets

These little projects are true scrap crafters. Once you get down to the smallest pieces of satin, a bit of calico, a piece of cotton that you might throw away, some lace, a tiny piece of ribbon, a few odd buttons, some leftover glitter, or those few strands of embroidery thread, here is where you'll use them up. As the ad says, "good to the very last drop."

A basket of sweet-smelling sachets is an addition to any sewing or lingerie display. They can be part of a booth as well. Hang them as ornaments on the Christmas tree. Some can have a perfume scent; others pine.

Materials Needed

Remnants of fabric and trimmings; needle and thread; absorbent cotton or batting; perfume (or pine needles, finely crushed).

Directions

Cut two matching pieces of fabric. They can be any shape: square, heart, round, or odd. Sew right sides together around edge, leaving opening to turn right sides out. Stuff loosely. If using cotton, scent with a drop of your favorite perfume. Sew opening closed. Trim with lace or ribbon. Design appliqué or embroidery as you wish.

Variations

Cut out small Christmas-tree shapes, a dove, and small stockings to make ornament sachets. Fill each with pine scents, and add a hanging loop of yarn. The trims are then made of all that glitters. Sequins, beads, glue-on glitter, and metallic threads are available in the five-and-ten and notions stores. Create one-of-a-kind ornament gifts. Sell them individually or in sets of four.

Making in Quantity

These are so easy to make that you won't save any time making them in quantity, but you will get more variety if several people pool material and creative talents.

When cutting out shapes, place several layers of fabric on top of each other, and see General Craft Tips, page 33, for cutting out patterns in quantity. Do all sewing at one time; then add trimmings. Working together on such projects is more for fun than efficiency.

Display Ideas

Old-fashioned tins found in novelty stores make delightful containers for display. Or small and odd-shaped baskets can be used. Don't overlook pretty bowls and dishes you may have around the house or ceramic and clay plant holders. Also see Berry Baskets on page 108.

Recipe for Potpourri

Potpourri is easy to make, looks pretty, and can be displayed in little drawstring fabric bags, clear Baggies tied with yarn, or ceramic pots.

Materials Needed

Fabric for sachets, a collection of dried rose petals, mint leaves, geranium, or lavender; orris root (a scent preservative available in most drugstores).

Directions

Collect rose petals, mint leaves, geranium petals when they are in full bloom. Dry them in a well-ventilated area. They can be spread on a pan in the sun, or for quick drying, I place my petals and leaves on a broiler pan and put them in a warm oven for about ten minutes. They are dry when they feel papery. You have to watch them because they will lose color if left too long.

You can also press fresh petals if you have a week to wait. Spread the petals on waxed or white bond paper, and put them under a stack of heavy books. Leave them alone until you're ready to remove them.

Crush petals and leaves, and mix them together in a clear apothecary jar. Add a few drops of orris root to retain the fragrance. It will take about a week for them to cure. Store in a dark place to retain color. Stir the mixture every few days. Spoon a bit of the potpourri into small bags that you make or buy. These can be sold as drawer fresheners.

Patchwork Place Mat

This is another scrap craft project made from larger pieces than the pincushions and sachets. Those used here are all from similar weights of cotton with bright summery colors and patterns. If you have scraps from this project, stitch up matching napkins. Not enough scraps? Make little cocktail napkins or coasters.

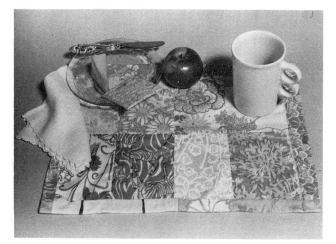

Materials Needed

8 pieces of 3½-x-5-inch scrap fabric; needle and thread; scissors; iron.

Directions

Sew four pieces of fabric together, right sides face to face with ¼-inch seams. You will have one 5-x-13-inch piece. Do the same with the other four pieces. Iron. Sew the two pieces together so you have one piece 9½ x 13 inches. Iron. Make a border of 1½-inch strips so that your finished mat measures 11 x 15 inches. Iron the finished project.

Variations

To make your mat reversible, sew two mats together around the edges with the right sides together. Leave an opening to turn right side out. Sew opening closed.

If you'd like to quilt the place mat, put a layer of polyester batting between the fabric, and quilt in a diamond pattern or two squares on each side of all seams.

Making in Quantity

As with all sewing projects, when making mats in quantity, cut and sew all pieces at one time. However, there is a lot of thread snipping on this project, and it helps to have one person check over each place mat as it is sewn.

Another precaution when making these in quantity: Try to keep the seams straight and accurate, or the place mat will be lopsided rather than perfectly rectangular.

Display Ideas

Create a setup using one place mat. If it is a bright pastel fabric, use casual props such as a picnic mug, plastic paper plates, an apple, springtime flowers. If the fabrics used are more elegant, try a bouquet of roses, a hand-lettered place card, a lace-trimmed napkin, and silverware. One setup will do even if you have a variety of place mats laid out on a table.

Paperback Book Cover

Once again, get out the scrap bag or go wild in the fabric shop. All it takes is a little bit of fabric, so look for remnants. Buy a variety of fabrics, patterns, and colors with contrasting trims, and before you know it, you'll have a cover for every paperback in the house. Select fabrics with different people in mind. Choose fabrics for different kinds of books. Floral patterns for a romance, dark suede for a mystery, a bandanna print for a western, a checked cotton to cover a crossword puzzle book. A plain brown can be stenciled with the words *Plain Brown Wrapper* and cover a spicy novel. It costs practically nothing to make this novelty item.

Materials Needed

1 piece of printed fabric 10½ x 8 inches; 1 piece of solid fabric 10½ x 8 inches; 2 pieces of solid fab-

ric 8 x 5 inches; 2 strips of printed fabric 11 x 2 inches; package of rickrack; needle and thread; scissors; iron; straight pins; safety pin; ⅝-inch grosgrain ribbon.

Directions

Turn larger pieces of fabric down ¼ inch on all edges, and press. Place wrong sides together, and pin. Turn the edges of the two 8-x-5-inch pieces in ¼ inch all around, and press. Fold each to create two pieces that measure 7½ x 2¼ inches each.

Place each of these pieces on the inside of each end of the larger piece. The folded sides will be in the center. Pin in place. (See drawing.)

Fold handle strips in half lengthwise with the right sides together. Stitch along length. Clip a

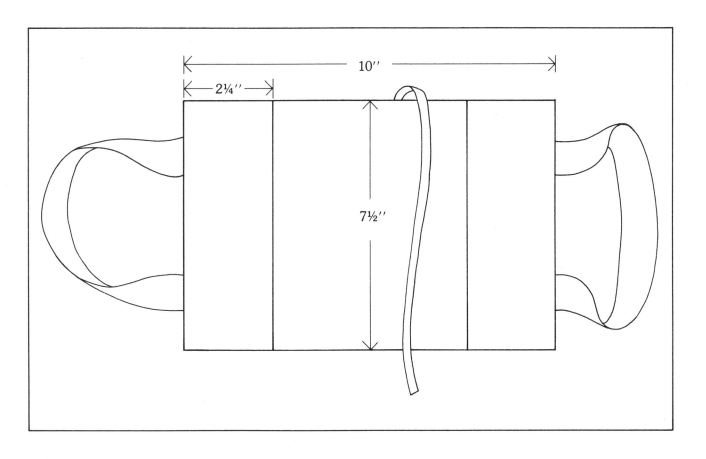

safety pin to the top of one edge. This will make it easy to turn fabric inside out. Remove pin. Press flat.

Measure 1¼ inches in from each edge, and attach handles between layers by pinning in place. Place a ⅝-inch grosgrain ribbon in the center of the book cover between layers of fabric. Cut the other end to an appropriate length for a bookmark.

Stitch all around the outside edges of the book cover, as close to the edge as possible. Press. Turn to the front, and pin rickrack trim all around the outside. Stitch in place.

Quick Crafts

The following projects are quick crafts. They are small and take very little time to make. None of them is intended to fill up a booth at a bazaar, but they are wonderful as inexpensive items for quick sales. Put them where they seem to fit. Display a sewing kit, for example, with pillows or other large sewing projects, where you know sewers will congregate. A little recipe holder sells well with recipe files, aprons, potholders, etc. Team up a crocheted star with other handmade Christmas ornaments. Make eyeglass cases from tote bag material (page 124). Sell these as matching sets.

All the projects are perfect last-minute gifts or stocking stuffers. Display idea: Make lots of different quick crafts, and display them in one booth called *Stocking Stuffers*. Determine the maximum price for the items, and keep your costs low.

Presto Baby Bibs

There is no work to making these quick and easy bibs for dressing up a baby, and planning the trim can be fun. Use up little bits of leftover ribbons, lace, etc., or buy a small amount of a number of trims. If you enjoy doing embroidery, choose one of the designs provided for other projects and apply it to this project.

Materials Needed

One dress shield (found in the five-and-ten); ribbons; trim; needle and thread; scissors.

Directions

No cutting—just trim, and presto! Use seam binding or ribbon around the neck, leaving enough to tie. Need a last-minute gift? Visiting a new mother in the hospital? Taking baby visiting to-

night? You can whip this up on the machine in less than a half hour.

Variations

Your imagination is the only limit. Sew ribbons together in strips. Make a basket weave of ribbons, Sew an appliqué to the front. Embroider an initial in one corner. Stencil baby's name in fabric paint.

Making in Quantity

Dress shields might be more expensive than is profitable for selling at a bazaar. Use pattern provided. Cut the bib shape from inexpensive cotton muslin, piqué, or polished cotton. You can cut out several at one time. (See General Craft Tips for cutting patterns in quantity.)

Display Ideas

If you have a baby, by all means use him or her to model the bibs. Take care of baby and business at the same time. Set up a high chair. The people passing by will be more than enough distraction. Change the bib often, depending on the number of designs you are showing.

No baby? Use several dolls as models. They will obviously be too small for the bibs, but they will look cute. Since the intention is not to be realistic, use any kind of doll or stuffed animal.

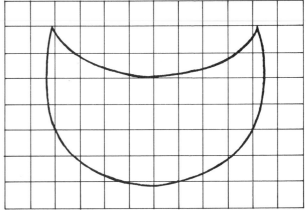

Dish Towel Apron and Potholder

It couldn't be easier to make the next two projects. This is made from a standard-size dish towel. The potholder is made from another dish towel, or you can use a piece of scrap fabric. The convenient feature of this project is that the potholder is attached with a small strip of Velcro, making it easy to remove, use, and reattach.

Materials Needed

1 dish towel; ¼ yard of matching fabric; two yards of 1-inch grosgrain ribbon; ¼ yard of cotton batting; package of Velcro; scissors; needle and thread.

Directions

Center the ribbon on one end of the dish towel and sew it on. This will create your waistband. Cut two 8-inch squares of fabric and two slightly smaller squares of cotton batting.

Place front of fabric pieces together and stitch around three sides. Turn inside out. Slip double layer of batting inside. Turn open edge in to form a hem and stitch closed. Quilt the potholder by stitching along the lines of the print or by sewing across the square, creating a checked pattern.

Sew a small piece of Velcro to one corner of the potholder. Sew another piece onto the apron. The potholder will stick to the apron for easy access.

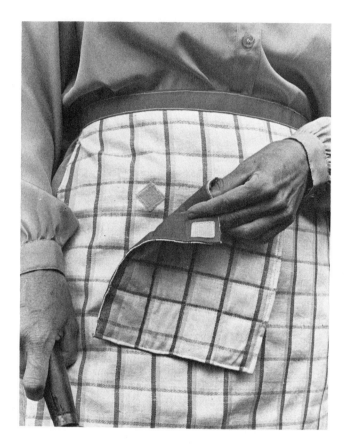

Variations

Make contrasting aprons and potholders combining different colors, fabrics, and patterns. You can choose a color scheme and stick with it for all items, or combine checks, polka dots, and stripes. Another idea is to use solid colors for the aprons with a patterned potholder to match the color.

Display Ideas

Of course, wear an apron at the bazaar. Change it often. Consider the clothes you wear so they go with the apron, or aprons, you will display. For example, if you have made aprons with a Christmas motif, wear party clothes to suggest that the apron is more than an everyday item. This will prompt people to consider it for a gift.

122

Child's Party Apron

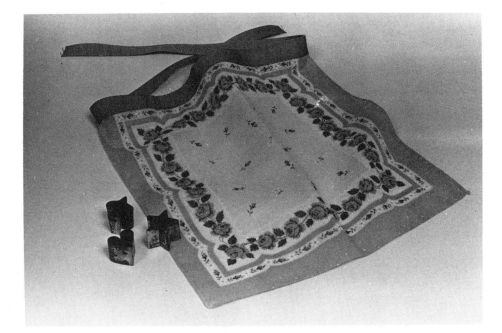

This project can easily be made in quantity and will be hard for anyone to resist buying. You will find colorful cotton handkerchiefs in the five-and-ten. Some have embroidery on a corner or around the edges, others are trimmed with lace, and some have overall printed patterns, such as the one shown here. The cost: three for $1. Add a yard of 1-inch-wide grosgrain ribbon stitched across the top edge, leaving enough on each side for tying.

Materials Needed

1 handkerchief; 1 yard grosgrain ribbon; iron; needle and thread.

Directions

Simply stitch the ribbon across the top edge and iron the completed apron.

Variations

These small, delicate party aprons can be made from little scraps for a patchwork design. Or add small presewn appliqués to the ribbon waistband. When a project is this easy to make, the material shouldn't be ordinary. Choose carefully. The soft colors and daintiness give this little item its appeal.

Display Ideas

To display them, always wear one. When you make it for yourself, you may need more ribbon for the ties. Tie several on a clothesline, or pin them to a backboard. If they are laid out on a table, it should be covered with pretty fabric or paper that won't detract from the designs. Consider folding each one neatly into a small hankie box. Add a flower stick-on seal to the top corner of each box. Who could resist such a darling gift?

Quilted Eyeglass Case

Make these eyeglass cases to match the lunch bags on page 49. You'll have enough material left over so it will cost nothing. Display them with sunglasses so that people who don't ordinarily wear glasses will be inspired to buy one. It's a handy gift as well as a practical item to own. The cases are fun to make because they are small, and the designs can vary with the material. Consider velvet and satin for evening wear. You might double sales.

Materials Needed

1 piece of fabric 8½ x 8 inches; 1 piece of fabric same size for lining; 1 piece of polyester batting same size; needle and thread; scissors; tape measure or ruler; pencil; white paper.

Directions

Use pattern to cut all material. Put the two pieces of fabric together, right sides facing. Place batting on top. Sew up each side and across the top. Leave the bottom open. Trim seams close to stitching. Turn the fabric for the outside over to the right side.

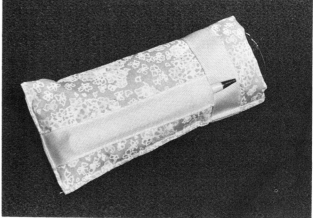

Quilt in diamond, square, or stripe pattern. Turn the bottom up to inside ¼ inch, and stitch. Fold in half. Topstitch sides and bottom.

Variation

Eyeglass Pen Case

Aside from the materials listed, you will need 15 inches of 1-inch-wide grosgrain ribbon. Add the ribbon to the fabric only, and do this before the lining and seams are stitched in place. Sew down both sides of the ribbon. Follow diagram, and leave an opening in the top of the vertical strip of ribbon to slip a pen into.

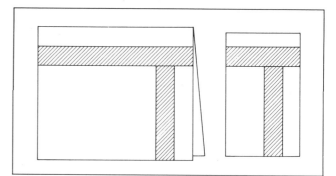

Map Case

Leatherlike vinyl cuts smoothly, needs no hemming, can be glued to itself, and is good-looking. Use it for making small travel items, key carrying case, luggage tags, and a car map case. The material takes acrylic paint well, and the items can be stenciled for personalized gifts.

Materials Needed

¼ yard leatherlike vinyl; wallpaper or ribbon or binding for the edges; white glue; scissors; ruler; pencil.

Directions

Cut a piece of vinyl 11 x 19 inches. Find the center of the short edges, and cut semicircles for pulling the map out. Fold sides over 4½ inches, leaving a gap of 1 inch in the center. Glue edges together.

Bind the edges with 1-inch-wide strips of wallpaper or 1-inch-wide ribbon. Coat the strips of wallpaper with clear nail polish.

Variations

Stencil the word *MAP* with acrylic paint and stencil sheet from the five-and-ten. Vinyl is available in a variety of colors and textures and comes 54 inches wide.

Making in Quantity

Make these in different sizes for different uses such as to hold a passport, credit cards, note pad. The color combinations you choose will determine who it might be for. Do all cutting and gluing at once. When stenciling, you can ensure a straight line by laying a piece of masking tape across or on the diagonal. Work along the straight edge of the tape, and remove when finished. Since you must wait for each letter to dry before going on to the next, you can work most efficiently on several projects at once.

Display Ideas

Cover a backboard with map cases in every color and design, or fill a basket so the customers can look through to pick the one they want. Vinyl takes handling well and won't soil if people are touching and looking.

Another way to display the brown vinyl is against a backboard that has been covered with a road map. Use self-adhesive stickers on the back of each case, and attach to board. These are easily removed as purchased.

Recipe Holder

This convenient little item is made with a small square bathroom tile, spring clothespin, paint, and glue. The decorations can be anything you want. Pictures, shells, pressed flowers, silhouettes, photos, initial—anything goes. It is perfect to clip a recipe to.

Materials Needed

1½-inch-square ceramic tile; Elmer's Glue-All; spring-type clothespin; acrylic or spray paint; decoration; clear nail polish (for making one), clear varnish (for making several).

Directions

Paint the clothespin in a color of your choice. You can leave the tile white or paint it to match the clothespin. Glue a design to the tile. The decoration can be a small paper design cut from wrapping paper or similar source. The photograph shown here will give you some ideas. Children's school photos fit perfectly on the tile if you need a quick gift for Grandma.

Glue the tile to the bottom of one side of the clothespin. If you have used paper for the design, coat it with clear nail polish. Do this to the clothespin as well. This will make it shiny.

Variations

I like to make these with pressed flowers. It takes a little more preparation time, but since the tiles are so little, there is only room for one buttercup, a leaf, or a few petals. One sheet of pressed material makes many projects. Leave an extra week for pressing. Once finished, the pressed items should be protected with a few coats of spray varnish.

Making in Quantity

Sheets of these tiles come on a paper backing. The major mail-order catalogs such as Sears and

J. C. Penney carry them. It is easy to cut them apart with scissors. When making a quantity, however, you can work on a sheet of twelve at one time and then cut apart.

Spray paint all clothespins in bright colors to go with the designs, or the other way around. You can make dozens in a day.

Display Ideas

They are displayed here on strips of glass that create shelving. In this way they can be lined up with all designs visible. These small items should be shown at eye level.

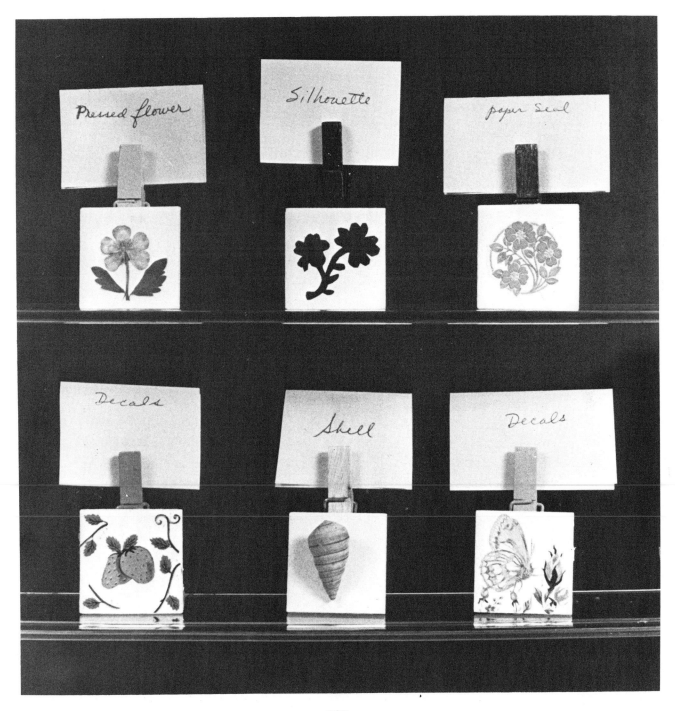

Sewing Aids

The two scissors-and-needle—holders were made from the leftover potholder material (page 122). They are cut to a convenient size to fit in a sewing box or purse. A button and looped ribbon are added for the closure. Each has a ribbon band on the inside for holding a small pair of embroidery scissors in place, and on the other side, a strip of red felt holds the pins. The whole thing is padded with cotton batting left over from other projects. They can be quickly stitched up on the machine or by hand. Use embroidery thread to make decorative stitches around the edges.

Buy inexpensive cloth tape measures in the five-and-ten, and dress them up with embroidery tape. Simply turn one end of the embroidery tape over one end of the measuring tape so that it covers approximately 1 inch on the underside. Stitch the tapes together so that the embroidery covers one side of the tape. This takes minutes on the sewing machine. Leave at least 1 inch for finishing off the other end in the same way.

Sew half of a snap on the inside of one end, and roll the tape up from the other end, forming a coil. Sew the other half of the snap at the correct point on the outside of the finished project.

Select a variety of embroidery tape to create a colorful display. Fill a basket, and watch these items walk away. Your time is minimal; the cost, limited to the tape measure, embroidery tape, and thread. Price accordingly. Great stocking stuffers for a sewing enthusiast. Suggest that anyone will find this a useful item to carry in a purse. There is always an occasion when we have to measure something and can use such a handy item.

Attention Getters

In the introduction to planning a bazaar I spoke about drawing cards. These are projects that get the customers' attention. They bring people into your area because they are clever, inexpensive, eye-catching, colorful, humorous, in motion, or in some way grab people. In some areas of the country it will be one thing, and in another part of the country something else. Sometimes it depends on the climate. This is where knowing your friends and neighbors in the community helps. According to people who make stuffed animals, nobody anywhere can walk by koala bears.

Miniature Roses

I have seen these little roses only once. Never before and never again, but I will not forget the sight. It was on the sidewalk in Greenwich Village in New York. There was a summer street fair, and a small dense crowd gathered around a woman who sat on a stool at the curb. In front of her was a large corrugated box filled with tiny ribbon roses in red, purple, yellow, pink, white, and even black. She was selling three for $1 (even in these inflationary times), and as fast as she could make them, a bunch of three was sold. She turned the ribbon expertly between her fingers, and it took real concentration to see how she did it. On this particular weekend she must have sold $3,000 worth of miniature ribbon roses.

I can't think of one single item in this entire book that typifies the perfect bazaar item, guaranteed to sell, more than this project. I'm sure there are many ways to display them, but in this case the roses make their own colorful display. There might be a way to make them in quantity, but if you can learn to turn a ribbon as fast as this woman did,

129

you will turn out more than enough for one bazaar. A word of caution; It takes several tries to get the knack of the turning, but keep trying. The results are worth it.

Materials Needed

Paper ribbon 1½ inches wide in a variety of colors: pink, red, peach, white, lavender, yellow (I can't recommend black, but that's up to you); ½-inch-wide floral tape; 24-gauge stem wire; very fine binding wire (30 gauge or finer); 1½-inch-long artificial rose leaf on a stem (see Source List); wire cutter or scissors.

Directions

Cut the 1½-inch paper ribbon 12 inches long (Photo 1). Roll the ribbon from one corner into a tight cone shape (Photo 2). Fold the ribbon away from you (Photo 3). Roll the cone toward you three revolutions. Fold ribbon away from you as in Photo 2 (Photo 4). Roll cone toward you two revolutions, and fold ribbon away as before.

Continue this process until the ribbon is used up. The rose shape will form as you roll and fold (Photo 5). With 3 inches of binding wire fasten a twist tie just below the rose blossom to prevent unfurling. Trim the excess wire with wire cutters (scissors can be used but are not as good).

(Photo 6) Cut stem wire to 6 inches, and attach the rose leaf and stem wire to the rose with 10 inches of floral tape. Wrap the tape around the stem all the way to the base.

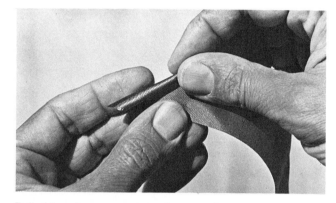

Roll ribbon from corner to make cone shape

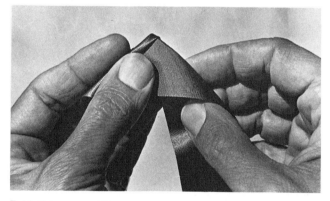

Fold ribbon away from you

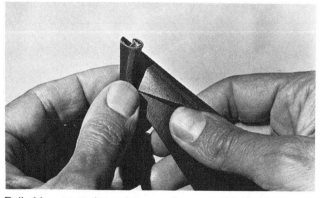

Roll ribbon toward you three revolutions and fold ribbon away from you as in photo #2

Roll and fold until ribbon is used up

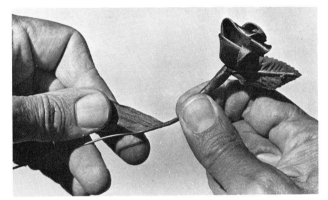

Starting just under blossom, wrap floral tape to bottom of stem wire

Twist tie edges with binding wire

Make minor adjustments in position of rose and leaf

Position rose leaf and stem wire for wrapping

Fuzzy Hand Puppets

The 10-inch-tall koala and lamb hand puppets are the original designs of Diane Babb, who owns Fuzzy Friends by Diane, a company that sells designs for making realistic stuffed animals. Diane's rabbit and fox arm puppets were featured in *Good Housekeeping* magazine, and her mail-order catalog is distributed all over the country. The designs are carefully thought out and more realistic than most patterns. They can be made quickly and take a minimum of experience or talent.

When showing at craft fairs, Diane always takes a large inventory as the puppets sell fast. "It's hard to say which sell best," she says. "The lambs, beavers, whales, koalas, walking bears, guinea pigs, mice, elephants, and pandas are equally popular. Sometimes it depends on the location, sometimes the mood of the crowd. But the biggest appeal is the realism of the designs."

It will take an average sewer less than an hour to make these small puppets, and Diane's customers compliment her on the simplicity of the directions.

The following patterns and directions are offered here with the permission of Diane Babb. (See Source List to order catalog of designs.)

Koala Bear Puppet

Materials Needed
(see Diane's comments on page 26)
Body
¼ yard of beige plush for body and face; small piece of white plush (3 x 8 inches) for chin gusset and ears (shaggy white fur may be used for the ears).

Eyes
1 pair of 15-millimeter brown eyes with safety lock.

Nose
1 30-millimeter koala nose with safety lock. (The eyes and nose are available from Fuzzy Friends by Diane.)

Directions

Use the pattern as indicated, and lay it to the back of your fur fabric. It is best to trace it to the fabric backing. Place the scissor blades against the backing so you won't cut the fur fibers. All seam allowances are ⅜ inch unless otherwise noted. *Do not cut the ear darts until instructed.*

Cut the back arms, front arms, head pieces, head gusset, body front, body back, and two ears from the beige fabric. Cut the chin gusset and two ears from the white fabric.

Match the head gusset to one head piece at the dot. Sew the head gusset to the head. Repeat with the other side. Make certain the ear darts line up evenly across from each other. If they don't, make an adjustment. Slash the ear darts.

Ears

With the right sides facing, match one white ear to one beige ear. Sew around the ear. Turn the ear to the right side. Repeat with the other ear pieces.

Insert the ear into the ear dart. Keep the white side to the front of the head. Sew across the dart, making certain that all raw edges are caught. Repeat with the other ear.

Chin

Match the chin to the head at the dot, continuing to match the chin to the head on both sides of the dot to the neck edge. Sew the chin to the head. Turn the head to the right side. Lay the head aside.

Body

With the right sides facing, match the back arms to the body back. See pattern piece for placement. Sew the arms in place.

Match the front arms to the front body in the same manner. Sew the arms in place. With the right sides together, match the front body to the back body. Sew from the top (neck) edge, around the arms and down the side. Repeat with the other side.

Finishing

Slip the turned head into the unturned body. Center the chin gusset to the center of the front body neck. Sew around the neck. Turn the entire puppet to the right side. Fold the raw edge at the bottom to the inside (½-inch turn), to form a hem. Sew the hem in place.

Pierce the fabric with the sharp tip of your scissors just above the chin gusset. Insert the nose, and lock in place. The eyes should be positioned 1 inch to the side of the nose and ½ inch up from the nose.

Lamb Puppet

Materials Needed

Body

¼ yard of acrylic lamb's-fleece fur.

Eyes

1 pair of 12-millimeter brown eyes with safety lock (the eyes are available from Fuzzy Friends by Diane); small amount of 3-ply black yarn for nose and mouth.

Directions

All seam allowances are ⅜ inch. Trace your pattern to the wrong side of your fur fabric. Cut as with the koala.

With right sides together match the front arms to the body front. Sew them in place. Match the back arms to the back body in the same manner, and sew the arms in place.

With the right sides facing, match the front body to the back body. Starting at the shoulder, sew the shoulder, around the arm and down the side. Repeat with the other side. Do not turn the body. Lay it aside.

Head

Match one under ear to one outer ear. Sew around the ear. Turn it to the right side, and gently pull the curved part of the under ear (raw edge) to match the straight edge of the outer ear. Stitch across. This will keep the ear in a curved downward position. Repeat with the other ear. Tack the ear to the head, as marked on the head pattern. Make certain that the curved edge faces the head.

Match the head gusset to one head at the dot. Sew the two pieces together. Match the remaining head to the head gusset in the same manner. Make certain the ears are properly caught as you sew. Match the center seam from the neck to the dot. Sew it closed. Turn the head to the right side.

Slip the head into the unturned body. Center the head by matching the center seam of the head to the center of the neck on the body. Sew the neck around. Turn the entire piece to the right side. Fold the bottom raw edge to the inside ⅓ inch, and sew a hem.

Finishing

Carefully pierce the head with the sharp tip of your scissors for the eyes. See the head pattern for placement. Position your eyes as close to the seam as possible. Insert the eye, and lock it in place. Make certain that the remaining eye will be positioned evenly across before you pierce the fabric.

Nose/mouth

Use a double strand of 3-ply yarn. Sew the mouth and nose as illustrated.

Fig. 1: 2 stitches across. Bring needle under the stitches.

Fig. 2: Pull the stitches down and insert the needle ¾ inch below.

Fig. 3: Bring needle back to the right side to form left half of the mouth. Return needle to inside at the center.

Fig. 4: Bring needle back to the right side to form the right half of the mouth. Return to the inside at the center. Tie off.

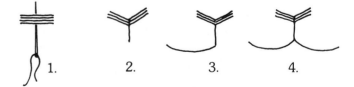

1.   2.   3.   4.

Making in Quantity

Since the fabric used for these projects is thick, it is difficult to cut more than one at a time. To make several, cut all pieces for each puppet, then do all stitching at one time. When all puppets have been sewn, finish with eyes, mouths, and noses.

Display Ideas

The hand puppets can be displayed on dowel stands or from a dowel "tree." Since they are so realistic and lovable, they don't need much to attract attention. If there is a background wall, hang a jungle or Peaceable Kingdom poster. One page in Diane's catalog shows a variety of puppets leaning over to read from Beatrix Potter's *The Tale of the Flopsy Bunnies.* It's adorable.

I once passed a store window filled with stuffed animals displayed in a chicken coop. It looked like a miniature cage. These are available by mail order (see Source List), and you might consider one for a display.

Koala Bear Puppet   Each square equals 1''

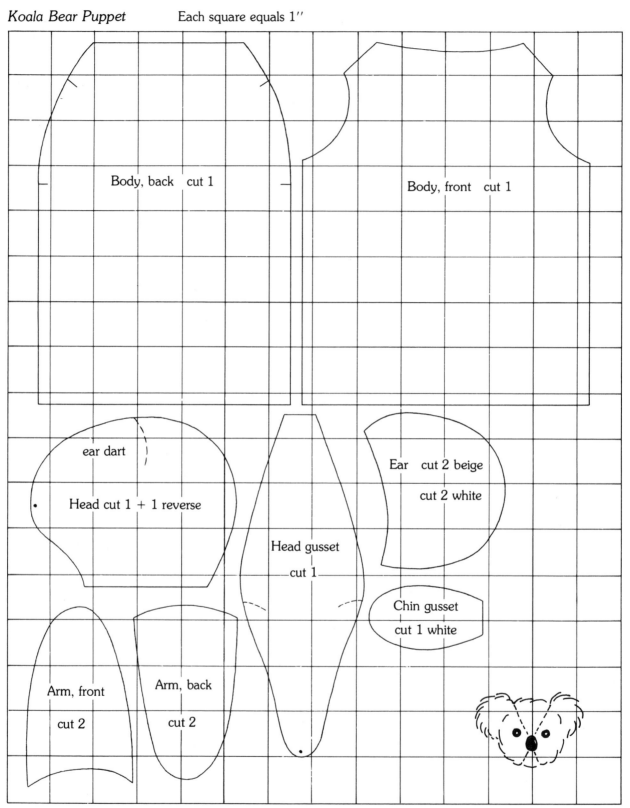

Body, back   cut 1

Body, front   cut 1

ear dart

Head cut 1 + 1 reverse

Head gusset

cut 1

Ear   cut 2 beige

cut 2 white

Chin gusset

cut 1 white

Arm, front

cut 2

Arm, back

cut 2

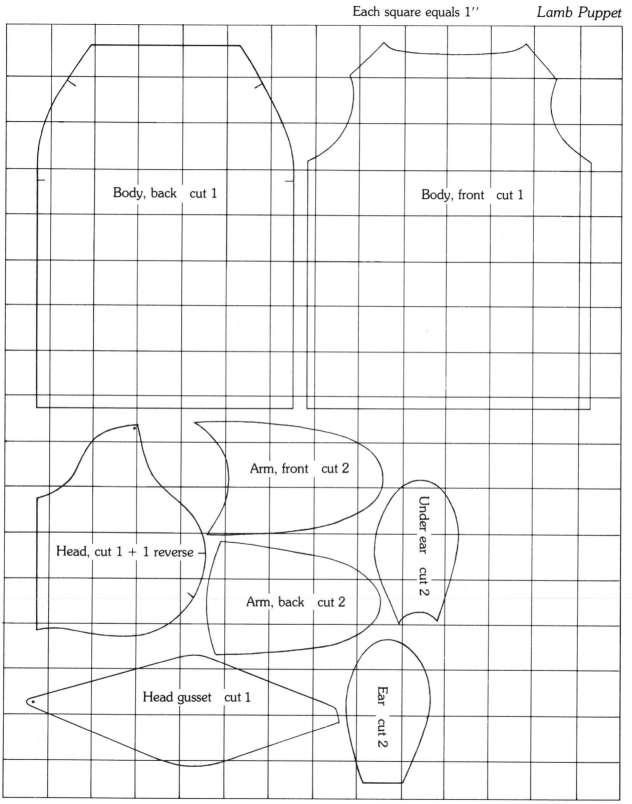

Body, back   cut 1

Body, front   cut 1

Arm, front   cut 2

Under ear   cut 2

Head, cut 1 + 1 reverse

Arm, back   cut 2

Head gusset   cut 1

Ear   cut 2

Bottles That Blossom

Freshen up bottles, tins, and throwaways. Start collecting early. Empty bottle? Or mayonnaise jar? Don't throw them away. Save them and get contributions from friends. Pretty apothecary jars are inexpensively priced. Use these, too. An orange juice bottle has never looked so good. This technique is decoupage in reverse and can be applied to an aspirin tin as well as to a clean bottle. Nothing here will look recycled. When you're finished, you may even be fooled yourself.

Materials Needed

A variety of empty jars and bottles that you can get your hand, or at least a fat-handled paintbrush, into; paper greeting cards; wrapping paper or wallpaper; cuticle scissors; Elmer's Glue-All; an assortment of acrylic paint; 1-inch sponge-type paintbrush.

Directions

Cut out paper designs for each bottle. Plan where you will place each cutout element before you begin to glue them in place inside the jar or bottle.

Dilute white glue with a drop of water. Spread this mixture over the front of the paper cutout, and insert it into the jar. Press the design against the glass from the inside. If this is difficult to do with your hand, insert a damp sponge applicator brush (inexpensive, in hardware stores), and press against the design. The excess glue will ooze out from the edges, but the glue will dry clear on the design. Remove excess glue from the inside of the glass by patting it with a damp sponge.

Let this dry for a few minutes. Select the colors (or mix) that best complement your designs. Paint the inside of each jar with acrylic paint. Let dry.

Add more paint, if needed, to fill in areas that are spotty. You'll get the best results if you dab the paint rather than brush it on.

These bottles should not be used to hold liquid because prolonged moisture will peel the paint away. To protect the painted finish, apply a coat of clear varnish over the inside of the bottle.

Variations

Make tins and boxes by painting the outside with acrylic paint. Let dry. Cut out paper designs, and glue them to the box or tin. Choose tiny stems, leaves, and buds for this. Coat small tins with clear nail polish until designs are sufficiently submerged. For larger items use clear spray varnish.

Dress Up a Bottle to Go Visiting

Who can resist something humorous? This project follows the rules for good bazaar crafting.

1. It is made with scraps. First came the apron, which gave birth to a potholder, which fostered this miniature cap, apron, and coasters.
2. It attracts attention.
3. It's not hard to identify (if modeled).
4. It can be made in no time flat; several, in three times that.
5. It enhances a bottle, and in this case, the outer wrap outlasts the gift.
6. It's irresistible at a bazaar.

Materials Needed

12 x 36 inches of fabric; double-folded bias tape (one package makes two sets); 3 inches of ⅛-inch elastic; needle and thread; scissors.

Directions

Refer to pattern, and cut one piece for the apron body. Cut one piece for the pocket. Cut two 4½-inch circles for the hat. Cut eight 3½-inch circles for the four coasters. No hems or seams are called for.

Pin pocket to fit at bottom of the apron. Sew bias tape around apron, adding about 3 inches to go around the neck of the bottle and attaching pocket to the apron.

Sew 7 inches of tape to each side of the apron to tie around the bottle.

Coasters

Pin two 3½-inch circles together so there are four circles. Sew bias tape around each circle.

Hat

Pin the two 4½-inch circles together. Sew a circle 2 inches from the center. Place elastic between the circles, close to the stitching. Pull enough to fit around the top of a bottle, and hand stitch the ends together. Stitch another circle so the elastic is within the casing. Sew the bias tape around the edge of the two circles, sewing them together. Slip over top of bottle for a floppy hat.

When you bring the bottle out all dressed up, it'll give everyone a laugh. Line them up in the kitchen or Christmas booth and have plenty in reserve. They will move quickly.

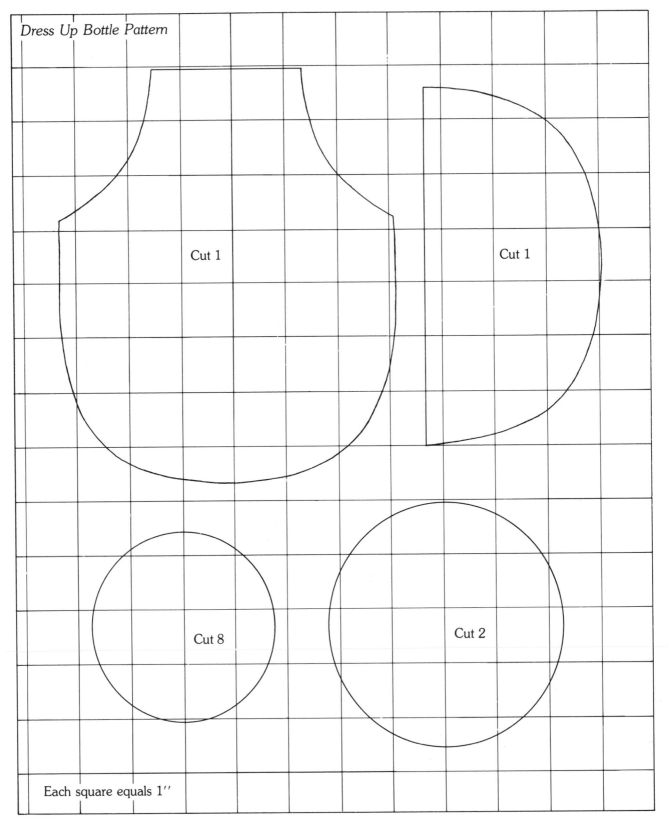

Dress Up Bottle Pattern

Cut 1

Cut 1

Cut 8

Cut 2

Each square equals 1''

Tissue Cover

What to do with the extra toilet tissue in the bathroom? Here is the perfect way to conceal it. I am told that this is one project that people love to make as well as buy, and everyone is attracted to them at bazaars.

Materials Needed

½ yard sheer fabric, such as dotted swiss, organdy, etc.; 1 yard of beaded lace or eyelet trim; needle and thread; scissors; 2 yards of ¼-inch velvet ribbon.

Directions

Cut one piece of fabric 7 x 16 inches. Hem the top edge, making a ½-inch casing to pull ribbon through. Make a narrow hem at the bottom of the fabric. Cut a 16-inch piece of eyelet, and thread the ribbon through it. Cut off excess. Cut another 16-inch length of eyelet, and thread 16 inches of ribbon through this.

Sew one length of trim to the bottom of the cover. Sew the other trim 2 inches from the top. Pull the remaining ribbon through the casing at the top.

With right sides together, sew the side seam from the bottom up. Do *not* sew through the casing. Turn right side out, pull the ribbon at the top, and slide a roll of tissue into the cover. Pull ribbon to cover paper at top, and tie in a bow.

Turtle Plant Holder

This clever item is shared by Anne Lane who designed it for her company, Anne Lane Originals. You may be familiar with her crochet designs as they have appeared in the magazines where her mail-order catalog of designs is offered. The turtle planter is made with knitted worsted over a small margarine container. It has a flower-bedecked turtle head and holds a small plant. Or it can be made more simply, without the turtle head. Anne Lane's customers report that these are always a hit on the plant table.

The patterns were designed for beginners. Their clarity and simplicity make them a constant winner with bazaar and craft show workers. Aside from the turtle plant holder, the bassinet purse and lapel pins are proved sellers. Other patterns are available for equally good projects. (See Source List for mail-order catalog.)

The directions and patterns are offered here by permission of Anne Lane Originals.

Materials Needed

8-ounce plastic margarine container; ½ ounce knitting worsted in desired color(s); Size F crochet hook for body; Size 00 crochet hook for head; 2 small wiggle eyes, or small black beads for eyes; small amount of red embroidery floss for mouth.

Directions

Body

Punch 24 holes evenly spaced around rim of margarine container. A standard paper punch works best for this.

Rnd 1: working from the inside out, make 2 sc in each hole around; join with a sl st.

Rnd 2: (work in back lps only) sc in each sc around; join with a sl st.

Rnd 3: ch 3 (to count as a dc), dc in each of next 3 sc, 2 dc in next sc. *dc in next 4 sc, 2 dc in next sc. Repeat from * around; join with a sl st.

Rnd 4: ch 3 (to count as a dc), dc in each of next 4 dc, 2 dc in next dc. *dc in next 5 dc, 2 dc in next dc. Repeat from * around; join with a sl st.

Rnd 5: ch 4 (to count as a dc, ch 1), skip 1 dc, *dc in next dc, ch 1, sk next dc. Repeat from * around; join with a sl st.

Rnd 6: end off body color, and join a trim color, in center of the first ch 1 sp ch 3 (to count as a dc), dc, ch 3 and sl st in 1st ch (pc made), 2 dc in same space. 1 dc in next ch 1 sp, *2 dc, pc, 2 dc in next sp, 1 dc in next ch 1 sp. Repeat from * around, join with a sl st, work in yarn ends.

Head

With white or trim color knitting worsted, ch 2.

Rnd 1: make 6 sc in 2nd ch from hook. Do not join rnds; carry a piece of contrasting color yarn be-

tween first and last sc to mark beg of rnds.

Rnd 2: inc in each sc around (12 sc).

Rnd 3: *sc in 1st sc, inc in next sc. Repeat from * around (18 sc).

Rnds 4−6: work even on 18 sc.

Rnd 7: *sc in first 4 sc, dec over next 2 sc. Repeat from * around (15 sc).

Rnds 8−12: work even on 15 sc. End off at end of rnd 12.

Flower Hat

With main color yarn and Size 00 hook, ch 5. Join with a sl st to form ring.

Rnd 1: *ch 4 sc on ring. Repeat from * 5 times.

Rnd 2: In each ch 4 lp make an sc, hdc, dc, hdc, sc. End off, leaving a 12-inch length of yarn for sewing.

Finishing

1. Stuff head firmly, and sew it to body through the punched holes, using neat overcast stitches.
2. Sew flower hat to top of head.
3. Embroider a smiling mouth.
4. Glue or sew on eyes.
5. Trim with anything else you want!

143

Bassinet Purse with Baby Doll

The following projects from Anne Lane Originals are the all-time number one sellers at bazaars and craft shows. Anne Lane says, "I have made hundreds of them, using pastel sports yarn crocheted over the bottom of a detergent bottle. It doubles as a little girl's purse and as a bed for a tiny doll. The doll pattern is included."

Bassinet Purse

Materials Needed

1 oval-shaped dish detergent bottle of 22- to 32-ounce size; 1 ounce sports yarn of desired color (Main Color, MC); ½ ounce sports yarn in a Contrasting Color (CC); small amount of white sports yarn; small amounts of blue, brown, and red embroidery floss; 1 12-inch square of white felt; small amount of stuffing, or several cotton balls; Size F crochet hook; Size 2 steel crochet hook; sharp knife, or other cutting tool; paper punch.

Directions

Cut off large end of detergent bottle 2½ inches up from bottom. Wash this and dry it thoroughly. With the paper punch make a row of holes around the top edge, spacing them approximately ½ inch apart center to center.

144

Skirt and Top of Purse

Rnd 1: join MC at narrow end of bottle; knot several times. With a Size F crochet hook make 3 sc in each punch hole around bottle; join to 1st sc with a sl st. Ch 1, and turn.

Rnd 2: (work in back lps only) sc in each sc around; join to 1st sc with a sl st. Ch 2, but *do not turn.*

Rnd 3: Make a hdc in each sc around; join to top of ch 2 with a sl st.

Rnds 4–5: repeat rnd 3.

Rnd 6: end off MC, join CC. Repeat rnd 3.

Rnd 7: end off CC, join MC. Repeat rnd 3; end with a sl st, ch 3.

Rnd 8: (beading rnd): *skip 1 st, dc in next hdc, ch 1. Repeat from * around; join to top of ch 3 with a sl st.

Rnd 9: (shell rnd): end off MC, join CC. Sl st to 1st ch 1 sp, ch 3 (to count as a dc), dc in same space, ch 2 and sl st in top of 2nd dc (pc made), 2 dc in same sp, dc in next ch 1 sp, *2 dc, a pc, 2 dc in next ch 1 sp, dc in next ch 1 sp. Repeat from * around; end off.

Hood

Starting at center of one of the narrow ends of the bottle, count off 8 sc on each side of center sc. Join MC to 8th sc on right side.

Row 1: ch 3 (to count as a dc). In front lps of *rnd 2* of skirt dc in 16 sc around end. Ch 1 and turn.

Row 2: sc in each sc around. Ch 1 and turn.

Rows 3 and 5: repeat row 1.

Rows 4 and 6: repeat row 2. End off at end of row 6.

Join CC to starting point of row 1. Starting there and working around edge of hood, make 3 sc in each end of a dc row, skipping the sc rows between each dc row. End off at opposite end of row 1, leaving a 10-inch length of yarn. Thread this in a yarn needle, and run it through each shell all the way around edge, gathering material into a hood shape. Fasten remainder of length securely at beginning of row 1.

Ties: Make 2

With a doubled strand of MC ch 55; end off. Run ties through beading rnd of skirt, one on each side.

Bassinet Cover

Place completed bassinet on square of white felt, and trace around bottom with a soft lead pencil. Leaving a ¼-inch margin outside of the pencil line, cut this out. Now mark off a strip of felt 12 inches long by 2½ inches wide; cut this out. Sew one edge of the strip around the edge of the oval-shaped piece; trim any excess length. Sew side seam. Slip covering over outside of bassinet; using overcast sts sew firmly to rnd 1 of skirt.

Baby Doll

Directions

Head

With white sports yarn and a Size 2 steel crochet hook ch 2.

Rnd 1: make 6 sc in 2nd ch from hook. Do not join rnds; carry a piece of contrasting color yarn between first and last sc to mark beg of rnds.

Rnd 2: inc in each sc around (12 sc).

Rnd 3: * sc in 1st sc, inc in next sc. Repeat from * around (18 sc).

Rnds 4–7: work even on 18 sc.

Rnd 8: *sc in 1st sc, dec over next 2 sc. Repeat

from * around (12 sc). Stuff head firmly before starting next rnd.

Rnd 9: dec 6 sc evenly spaced around (6 sc). End off, leaving a 12-inch length for sewing.

Arms and Legs: Make 2
   With MC ch 40.

Row 1: make 3 sc in 2nd ch from hook and in rem 38 ch; end off. Twist completed piece into a spiral.

Dress
   Front of Bodice
With MC ch 7.

Row 1: sc in 2nd ch from hook and in 5 rem ch (6 sc). Ch 1 and turn.

Rows 2—4: work even on 6 sc. End off at end of row 4.

   Back of Bodice
Work as for front of bodice, but *do not* end off at end of row 4; ch 1 and turn.

   Skirt

Rnd 1: sc in 6 sc of back of bodice, ch 2, sc in 6 sc of front of bodice, ch 2 and join to 1st sc of back of bodice with a sl st. Mark end of rnd as for head.

Rnd 2: sc in each sc, and ch around (16 sc). Mark end of rnd as for head.

Rnd 3: *sc in 1st sc, inc in next sc. Repeat from * around (24 sc).

Rnd 4: end off MC, join CC. In 1st sc ch 3 (to count as a dc), dc in same sc, ch 2 and sl st in top of 2nd dc (pc made), 2 dc in same sc; sk next 2 sc. *In next sc make 2 dc, a pc, 2 dc; sk next 2 sc. Repeat from * 6 times (8 shells total). Join to ch 3 with a sl st; end off.

Hat
   Rnds 1—3: with MC work as for head.

Row 4: sc in first 12 sc. Ch 1 and turn.

Rows 5—7: Work even on same 12 sc. Ch 1, and turn at end of each row, except at end of row 7 end off.

Row 8 (border and tie row): with CC ch 20, join yarn to and sc in 1st sc of row 7, sc in remaining 11 sc of row 7, ch 20, end off.

Assembly

   Place the two arm and leg spirals side by side, and sew firmly several times through the 4th twist from the top. The top three twists are the arms; the rest are the legs. Sew the head on firmly at the junction of the two spirals. Slip the dress on over the legs, and sew each side at the shoulders. With blue embroidery floss make two french knots for the eyes; with red embroidery floss make a mouth. At top of head with desired color embroidery floss or yarn make three or four ½-inch-diameter loops for hair. Tie hat under chin and sew it on if desired.

Abbreviations

MC = Main Color
CC = Contrasting Color
ch = chain
sc = single crochet
dc = double crochet
hdc = half double crochet
sl st = slip stitch
rnd = round
yo = yarn over
lp(s) = loop(s)
inc = increase
dec = decrease
to inc - work 2 sc in the same sc
to dec - draw up a lp in 2 consecutive sc; yo and through all 3 lps on hook

Lapel Pins

Anne Lane calls these crochet designs Quickies because they can be crocheted by the dozen from leftover yarn. Included are patterns for a clown, turtle, ladybug, and mouse.

Some of Anne Lane's customers are senior citizens. They use the lapel pin patterns and a larger hook to make sachets and pincushions for friends. One ingenious senior stuffed the mouse with catnip and said it was the best catnip mouse her cat *ever* had.

Pins

Materials Needed

Specific materials for each pin will be indicated in the pattern for that pin. You will need *in addition* to the specific materials the following: Size 00 crochet hook; small amounts of stuffing; safety pin, approximately 1 inch long; extra-strong carpet thread to sew safety pin on with.

Lady Bug Pin

Materials Needed

10 yards of red knitting worsted; 10 yards of black knitting worsted; small amounts of white and black embroidery floss.

Directions

Top of Body

With red knitting worsted, ch 2.

Rnd 1: make 6 sc in 2nd ch from hook. Do not join rnds; carry a piece of contrasting color yarn between first and last sc to mark beginning of rnds.

Rnd 2: inc in each sc around (12 sc).

Rnd 3: work even on 12 sc.

Rnd 4: *sc in 1st sc, inc in next sc. Repeat from * around (18 sc).

Rnd 5: Work even on 18 sc. End off, leaving a 12-inch length of yarn for sewing.

Bottom of Body

With black knitting worsted, ch 2.

Rnds 1−2: repeat rnds 1−2 for top of body.

Rnd 3: *sc in 1st sc, inc in next sc. Repeat from * around (18 sc).

Rnd 4 (for legs): sc in 4 sc, * (sc in next sc, ch 4, sc in same sc), sc in next sc, repeat between () **, sc in 4 sc, repeat from * to **, sc in last sc. End off.

Finishing

1. Sew top of body to bottom of body, stuffing firmly before opening becomes too small.
2. With black knitting worsted, embroider a head and a stripe down the back. Scatter embroidered spots across top of body.
3. For the eyes, using white embroidery floss, make two straight vertical stitches; cross them with two horizontal stitches, using black embroidery floss.
4. Sew safety pin firmly to bottom of body.

Turtle Pin

Materials Needed

10 yards of green knitting worsted; 20 yards of white knitting worsted; small amounts of black, red, and yellow embroidery floss.

Directions

Top of Body

Using green knitting worsted, work as for Ladybug Pin.

Bottom of Body

Using white knitting worsted, work as for Ladybug Pin until rnd 3 is completed.
Rnd 4: sc in 4 sc (sc, ch 5, sc in next sc), sc in 3 sc, repeat (), sc in 4 sc, repeat (), sc in 3 sc, repeat (), sc in last sc. End off.

Head

With white knitting worsted, ch 2.
Rnd 1: make 6 sc in 2nd ch from hook. Do not join rnds; mark as for top of body.
Rnds 2–5: work even on 6 sc. End off at end of rnd 5, leaving a 12-inch length of yarn for sewing.

Finishing

1. Sew top of body to bottom of body, stuffing firmly before opening becomes too small.
2. Stuff head, and sew to front.
3. With white knitting worsted make 5 "lazy daisy stitch" petals over 3 rnds of back for a flower; using yellow embroidery floss, make a french knot in the center of the flower.
4. Using black embroidery floss, make two french knot eyes on either side of head; with red embroidery floss, make a smiling mouth.
5. Sew safety pin firmly to bottom of body.

148

Mouse Pin

Materials Needed

20 yards of gray knitting worsted; small amounts of pink and black embroidery floss.

Directions

Body Pattern

With gray knitting worsted, ch 2.

Rnd 1: make 6 sc in 2nd ch from hook. Do not join rnds; mark as for top of body in Ladybug Pin pattern.

Rnd 2: work even on 6 sc.

Rnd 3: *sc in 1st sc, inc in next sc. Repeat from * around (9 sc).

Rnd 4: work even on 9 sc.

Rnd 5: *sc in first 2 sc, inc in next sc. Repeat from * around (12 sc).

Rnd 6: work even on 12 sc.

Rnd 7: *sc in first 3 sc, inc in next sc. Repeat from * around (15 sc).

Rnds 8–11: work even on 15 sc.

Rnd 12: *sc in first 3 sc, dec over next 2 sc. Repeat from * around (12 sc).

Rnd 13: *dec over first 2 sc. Repeat from * around, being careful to stuff body firmly before opening becomes too small. Draw remaining sc together, and fasten securely, leaving a 4-inch length of yarn for the tail.

Ears: Make 2

With pink embroidery floss, ch 2.

Rnd 1: Make 5 sc in 2nd ch from hook. End off.

Finishing

1. Sew ears to head at rnd 4 of body.
2. With black embroidery floss, make two french knot eyes.
3. Run a double strand of white carpet thread through nose several times between 1st and 2nd rnds for whiskers.
4. With pink embroidery floss, embroider a satin stitch nose.
5. Sew safety pin securely to underside of mouse.

149

Clown Pin

Materials Needed

10 yards of multicolored knitting worsted; 10 yards of pink knitting worsted; 4 yards of white knitting worsted; small amounts of black and red embroidery floss.

Directions

Head

Starting at top of head, with pink knitting worsted ch 2.

Rnd 1: make 6 sc in 2nd ch from hook. Do not join rnds; mark as for top of body in Ladybug Pin pattern.

Rnd 2: inc in each sc around (12 sc).

Rnd 3: *sc in first 2 sc, inc in next sc. Repeat from * around (15 sc).

Rnds 4–5: work even on 15 sc.

Rnd 6: dec 3 sc evenly spaced around (12 sc).

Rnd 7: stuffing head firmly before opening becomes too small, dec 6 sc evenly spaced around. End off pink knitting worsted, and join multicolored knitting worsted.

Rnd 8: ch 3 (to count as a dc), make 2 dc in same space. *make 3 dc in next sc. Repeat from * around. End off multicolored knitting worsted, and join white knitting worsted.

Rnd 9: make 2 sc in each dc around. End off; fold yoke in half, and stitch together in center.

Hat

With multicolored knitting worsted, ch 2.

Rnd 1: Make 6 sc in 2nd ch from hook. Do not join rnds; mark as for *head*.

Rnd 2: Work even on 6 sc.

Rnd 3: Inc in each sc around (12 sc).

Rnd 4: Work even on 12 sc.

Rnd 5: * sc in 1st sc, inc in next sc. Repeat from * around (18 sc).

Rnd 6: work even on 18 sc. End off multicolored knitting worsted, and join white knitting worsted.

Rnd 7: (work in back lps only) make 2 sc in each sc around. End off, leaving a 12-inch length of yarn for sewing.

Finishing

1. Sew hat to head.
2. With black embroidery floss, make two crosses for eyes.
3. With doubled red embroidery floss, embroider a nose and mouth.
4. Sew safety pin securely to back of hat.

150

Decorative Accessories

In this section you'll find a variety of general craft projects that have gift appeal as well as being useful and decorative for the home.

The projects will suggest a variety of booths that you might set up. For example, a kitchen booth can accommodate a multitude of items that can be designed for kitchen uses. If you know what each person enjoys working on, you might suggest designing the projects so they are coordinated.

When creating things for the home, have a wide variety of colors. In this way, if someone wants to buy an item, he or she won't be turned away if the color doesn't fit the room scheme.

If you choose to work on light-switch plates, for example, design them for various rooms in a house. Some might also be made for a single switch, while others should fit a double.

Hanging Hearts

Elmer's glue and food coloring are the basis for these hanging hearts. The light shines through, and they sway gently in an open window. It is a bedroom ornament or can be hung as a mobile over baby's crib.

Make them in pink, green, yellow, or orange. Edge each one with a daisy chain trim and embroidered ribbon.

Materials Needed

Masking tape; tracing paper; plastic wrap (such as Saran); TV antenna wire; ball-headed pins; Elmer's Glue-All; red food coloring; lace ribbon.

Directions

A worktable with a surface that you can stick pins into is needed. Make three hearts, 6 inches, 5 inches, and 4 inches wide, by tracing them from the patterns provided. Tape the heart tracings to the work surface.

Next, tape a piece of plastic wrap over each tracing, leaving 2 inches of plastic wrap extending all

around. Pin the TV antenna wire on its edge, around the heart shapes. Tape the wire ends together where they meet.

Pour the glue into the heart shapes until it covers the surface to a depth of a shirt cardboard. Drop red food coloring into the glue in different spots. The color will spread and create a pinkish cast to the hearts.

Let the hearts dry for two days or until hard. When the wire is removed, the glue hearts should be as hard as plastic. Remove the plastic backing by peeling it away from the heart.

Finish off the edges of each heart by gluing a daisy chain of lace around each. Make a bow in the center top of each one, and connect them together for hanging.

Making in Quantity

This is difficult to make in quantity if you don't have plenty of room. Once you have the setup, however, it is as easy to make several as it is to make one. Trace the hearts as often as needed, get all molds ready, and pour the glue into as many as you need.

Display Ideas

The hearts should be hung to be appreciated. Don't hang them against a solid wall. Light should shine through. Hang them so they can swing freely.

To gift wrap, line flat boxes with heart-shaped paper doilies, and tie each box with heart ribbons. Use heart seals. Heart motifs are all around. Use this as the theme for your booth.

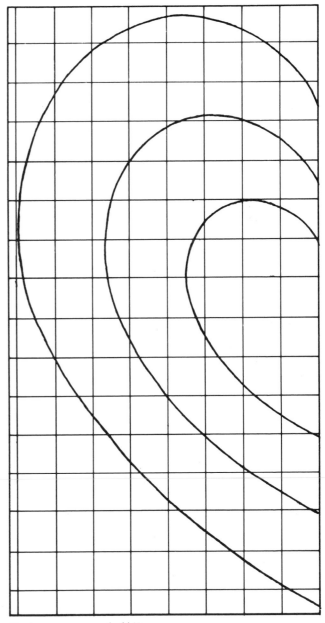

Each square equals ½''

153

Flower Arrangements

There are many different ways to make the flowers used for arrangements. You can dry real flowers, make artificial ones from fabric, crepe paper, foil, and tissue paper, or buy the individual parts and put them together quickly and easily. I decided to choose the latter so that the crafting time and talent could be spent on the arrangements themselves.

Flower arrangements seem to be included as a standard booth at bazaars. At the last one I attended this booth was a terrific sellout. Perhaps part of the reason was that the bazaar took place on the Saturday before Mother's Day. The floral arrangements were large, small, all colors, styles, variations, and prices. The containers were just as varied—teacups, mugs, baskets, bowls, vases, ceramic eggcups, and inexpensive novelties.

The sign read "Remember Mother's Day," and each bouquet included a decorative greeting card. Some of the arrangements sported lavish ribbons and plump bows. Some combined dried flowers with the artificial ones. If you have a talent for arranging flowers, this is the perfect craft for you.

While some craft shops, five-and-tens, and floral shops sell the parts to make the artificial flowers, I found a company in Florida, Enterprise Art (see Source List), that supplies everything you will need.

The mail-order catalog is extensive, and the prices are reasonable, making it possible to resell the items at an equally reasonable price.

Making in Quantity

This is the only sensible way to make the flowers and Michael Cousin at Enterprise Art will give your group a discount for ordering in quantity.

Flower parts are available in a variety of sizes and styles

154

Lined Baskets

Baskets are versatile and inexpensive. They are found in the five-and-ten, plant shops, and novelty stores, as well as through mail-order sources. In order to make ordinary baskets more attractive, line them with fabric.

If you are selling these baskets at a bazaar, display a few as they might be used. Do not leave it up to the customer's imagination. Show off your projects to their best advantage.

Since each basket is different, precise measuring is almost impossible. Cut the pieces of fabric as accurately as possible, and plan to tack the lining in the basket once it is in place. Roll the edges of the fabric over the edge of the basket, and tack here and there.

Attach ribbons, artificial flowers, and fruit to the sides or handle of each basket. This will add to its appeal.

Decorator Light Switch Plates

Metal and wooden light switch plates come in single and double sizes and are much nicer than the plastic ones. They can be designed to go in any room in anyone's house and in every color scheme you can think of. Because the area to design is small, it is easy and fun to create a variety of elaborate or simple motifs.

Materials Needed

Light switch plate: if wooden, acrylic paint; if metal ones are used, they will probably be painted white; brush (for painting); cuticle scissors; paper design to be cut out (cards, wrapping paper, silhouettes, book pages); glue; sponge; Krylon clear spray varnish.

Directions

Paint light switch plate if needed. Select a design that will fit on the area, and cut it out. One of these is from a Kate Greenaway paper book; the other is a silhouette from Geecraft (see Source List). Glue the paper design in position, and pat down firmly with a slightly damp sponge. This will remove any excess glue.

Spray a coat of clear varnish over surface. Let it dry, and recoat several more times until the design is well protected.

Embroidered Tea Towels

Buy inexpensive linen towels, or make your own. It's a simple project that requires cutting, hemming, and straight stitching. The embroidery designs can be as elaborate as you like, but I prefer a simple shaft of wheat or grasses and a lily pad for each. If there is too much embroidery, the towel can't be used and becomes impractical for a bazaar item.

Sewing tip: If your embroidery thread gets tangled, separate and lay out what you need for your project. Make a long braid, and pin it to the fabric or canvas you are working on. When you need a color, pick it out with your needle, and pull it away from the braid.

Materials Needed

Golden brown thread for the wheat design, brown and green threads for the other; needle; scissors; embroidery hoop; steam iron; damp towel.

Directions

Use the guide for embroidery stitches. Trace and transfer the design to the material. Place the embroidery hoop over the area to be worked so that the fabric is taut. Linen has a lot of give and requires repositioning in the hoop from time to time as you work it.

Don't knot the thread. Leave it loose on the underside of the fabric, and don't pull the stitches too tightly. Start and finish all ends by running them under the previous stitches on the wrong side.

When the embroidery is complete, turn the towel over onto a padded ironing board. Place a damp towel on top of the back of the embroidery, and press with a steam iron.

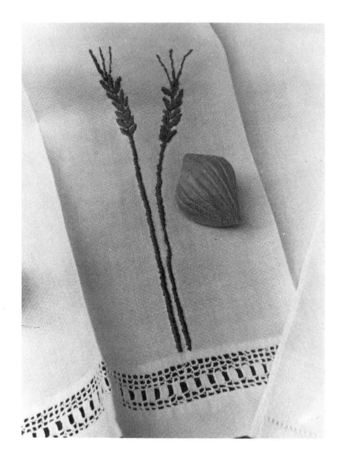

Variations

There are many designs that can be applied to this project. It's such fun to create a painting with needles and thread that sometimes we do it for ourselves rather than as a gift or for a bazaar. In this case it doesn't matter how long it takes or how intricate the design. Choose any of the patterns supplied in the book. Perhaps one of the designs meant for a stenciled box (page 68) will suit you, or the designs created for the baby pillow project (page 85).

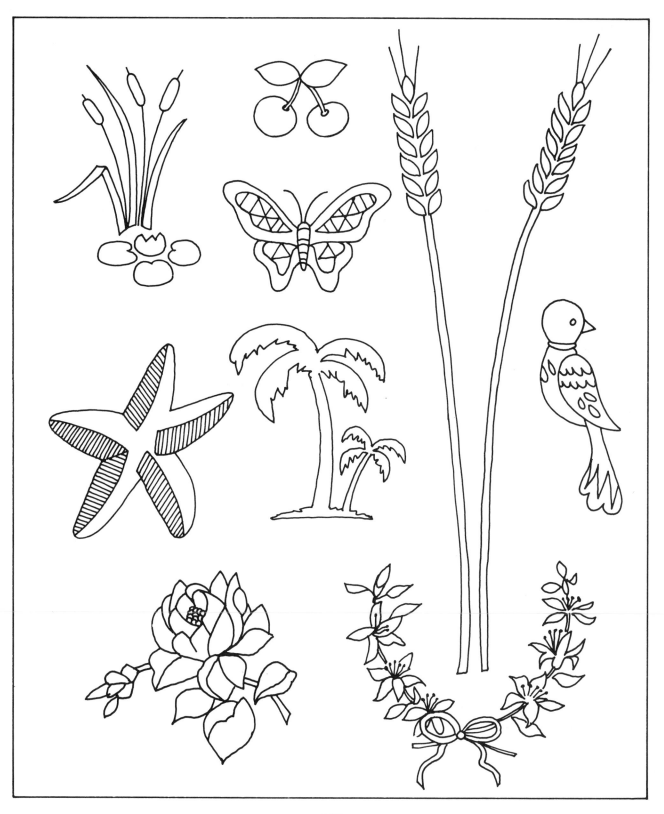

Mini Picture Plaques

The technique used to make these plaster picture plaques is a takeoff on decoupage. The tedious cutting is eliminated, but the finished project is no less beautiful. Lynn Brunhuber makes these picture plaques to sell at fairs, and she says all the teen-agers buy them for their rooms. They usually sell for $5 and $6 and make wonderful Christmas gifts. The sizes vary according to the molds used to make them. Lynn makes her own plaster plaques to decorate but says they are available ready-made in craft shops.

Materials Needed

Cards or wrapping paper (with white background); molds and plaster or ready-made plaques (craft shops); 1 bottle of Decal-It (available in craft shops); 1 jar of Mod Podge mat finish (craft shop); #400 and #600 Wetordry sandpaper by 3M; sponge applicator (small size); cuticle scissors; clear acrylic sealer or Mod Podge glossy finish; felt for backing on plaque; picture hanging tab for back.

Directions

While decoupage involves cutting out pictures from paper, this technique involves making a decal from existing designs. Select cards or wrapping paper with pictures that you like and will fit nicely on the plaques.

Lynn has several different-shaped plastic molds into which she pours the plaster to make her own plaques. The molds to make these are available in craft shops but are more difficult to find than the ready-made plaques.

The directions on the bag will tell you how to mix the plaster. When making your own, let the plaster set for one hour; then remove it from the mold. Let this dry for three days or longer.

The card or wrapping paper you use should not be made of parchment paper, and photographs won't work. Lynn reminds us that it's very important to use a picture with a white background.

Turn the picture into a decal according to the directions on the bottle of Decal-It. When ready, cut around the picture, but it needn't be as close as with decoupage.

Apply a thin coat of Mod Podge mat finish to the plaque, and affix your decal. Smooth it down with your fingers, so there are no bubbles or wrinkles. Let this dry for fifteen to twenty minutes.

Apply four coats of Mod Podge at fifteen- to twenty-minute intervals. This seals the design on the plaque. The last coat must dry thoroughly; then sand lightly with #400 wet sandpaper. Allow to dry. Continue to apply Mod Podge and sand eight or ten times until the desired finish is achieved. It will become smooth and silky.

Apply a coat of clear acrylic sealer for a glossy finish. Let dry. Place each plaque on a piece of felt, draw around it, and cut this out. Glue to the backs of each, and add a tab for hanging.

Making in Quantity

Lynn recommends working on many at one time since you have to wait for them to dry between each application.

Display Ideas

"When I take this craft to a bazaar or craft show, I set up a table and display them on small easels made from curtain hooks. They can also be hung on the wall," Lynn says. Or cover a backboard with delicate wallpaper or wrapping paper to make a wall display.

161

Ribbon Box

This is another way to decorate a plain wooden box. Make one for yourself in a color to match a particular room, or plan to create a beautiful display with boxes done in rainbow colors. The bow is made of stiff paper and will not lose its shape. The only real expense here is the box, which is available in all sizes and prices at most craft shops.

Materials Needed

A 5-x-5-x-4½-inch wooden box; heavy white paper such as bristol board; Elmer's Glue-All; pale blue spray paint; clear acrylic spray such as Krylon; cotton fabric for lining (or plan to paint inside); straightedge; razor.

Directions

Spray paint the box with two or three coatings, or until it is evenly painted.

Cut two strips of bristol board 14 inches long by ⅞ inch wide. If you cut against the grain, it will be easy to curl and fold. To determine which way the grain goes, curl the large piece of bristol board. It will bend easier along the lines of the grain.

Glue the strips both ways across the top and down the sides so it looks as if they go completely around the box as a real ribbon would. Cut another strip 8½ inches long. Form the bow by shaping the paper strip with your thumb and forefinger. It will curve as you direct it. Glue the ends of the bow shape together in the middle (see diagram). Cut a piece 3 inches long by ¾ inch wide to fashion the crosspiece of the bow. Glue it around the middle of the bow. Cut a strip 2 inches long by ⅞ inch wide to make the bow ends. Cut a **V** shape out of one end of each strip, and fashion an **S** curve to follow the bottom of the bow. Glue to the bottom of the bow. Glue the completed bow to the intersection of white strips on the box.

Dilute the glue with a few drops of water. Paint over the entire bow with this solution. The bow will dry very hard. Spray with acrylic coating to protect the surface of the painted box and the paper bow.

Paint the inside of the box, or line it with cotton fabric of a contrasting color and pattern. Attach fabric with the glue. Add a piece of fabric to the bottom.

Variations

You can make many different shapes with the curved paper and glue. Create flower petals or other curved designs to place on top of small boxes. If you make bows for the top of the trinket boxes (page 55), create a band of paper ribbon around the base of the bottom. Each will look like a tiny old-fashioned bandbox.

Making in Quantity

Spray paint several boxes in a variety of ice-cream colors: raspberry, vanilla, chocolate, blueberry, pistachio, lemon and orange sherbet.

If all the boxes are the same size, you can measure and cut the paper as one long strip to be cut at measured intervals. One person can do all the cutting, while another glues the strips in place. Someone else can make bows while another glues each in place on the top of each box.

When working alone, make all the bows first because they take more time than the other steps.

Display Ideas

Set items into or around each box suggesting its use. Keep everything light and delicate in keeping with the design and colors of these boxes. Use ribbons in pastel colors and varying widths to create displays. Drape them; tie them together; arrange them coming out of the boxes.

Glue under   Glue under   Completed bow

Wrap around bow

Porcelain Flowers

Inexpensive plastic flowers from the five-and-ten are the basis for this project. They are simply coated with Krylon white spray paint and arranged in interesting containers. It is so easy to do, and the variations you can create are only as limited as the flowers you can find. Any type, color, or size flower can be used.

Materials Needed

A can of Krylon white spray paint; plastic foam blocks to hold flowers; a selection of plastic flowers; scissors; containers to hold bouquets.

Directions

Select enough flowers for each bouquet. Flowers that come as a cluster or have many blossoms on one stalk can be cut apart to create a fuller arrangement. Stick the individual flowers in blocks of plastic foam, and spray paint. Keep moving the can back and forth as you spray so that you won't overload one area. You may have to approach the flowers from above, under, and inside in order to coat them thoroughly.

There should be no color showing. Let them dry. Repeat if needed. Remove the flowers from the plastic foam, and arrange them in selected containers.

Variations

The flowers will dictate the variations that are possible, but the process is the same. Whatever you use, the effect will be the same; however, the smaller blossoms look more like porcelain than the larger ones.

Porcelain Frame

The frame is made in the same way as the flowers. Once you have all the flowers painted and ready for an arrangement, save a few to make a matching frame. This is a dime-store variety, and it is simply spray painted white. The flowers are glued to the top and bottom with Elmer's Glue-All. The flowers and frame make a pretty combination set. Display them together, and add accessories to show it off.

Making in Quantity

The project lends itself to making in quantity. You can spray paint as many flowers as you can line up. Once they are dry, you will have all you need to make up one arrangement after another.

Display Ideas

Select containers that are equally inexpensive in order to keep your cost low. A pretty teacup with a delicate design can be found in the five-and-ten. Baskets in all sizes and shapes, a bowl, tin mugs, a pitcher are some suggestions. You can spray the baskets white also or leave them natural for contrast. A red tin mug, for example, offsets the white porcelainlike flowers, whereas a china teacup suggests another mood.

Fantasy Finish Frames

These picture frames are simple woodworking projects, and the finish is created with food coloring and Elmer's glue to look like marble. You can use an existing wood picture or mirror frame.

Everyone has photographs to frame, so plan to make several different sizes to fit standard photos. It's easy enough to experiment with the marbleizing technique, and you'll want to create different patterns and combinations of color.

Materials Needed

Elmer's Glue-All; a can of Krylon crystal clear acrylic; ⅜-inch velvet ribbon; ¼-inch balsa wood strip (the amount of ribbon and balsa wood to be determined by the size of your frame); toothpicks; watercolor paints or food coloring; ¼-inch plywood (4 x 7 inches for the large frame, 3½ x 3½ inches for the smaller frame, 9 x 9 inches for the heart); framer's easel back or cardboard to make small stand in back of each; saber or jigsaw (depending on type of frame); lace and rickrack for heart-shaped frame.

Directions

If easel backs are used, cut plywood frame shape to fit. If you will make your own stands, the frames can be any shape or size. Use a saber saw to cut the opening in the frames to fit common picture sizes. The heart-shaped frame is cut on a jigsaw. Sand all edges smooth.

Fantasy Finish

The fantasy finish resembles marbleizing and is created with two contrasting colors of glue paint. Mix together ¼ cup of glue and ¼ teaspoon of watercolor paint or food coloring. Add more color if a darker color is desired. Apply the glue paint to the frame by either pouring or spreading it over the surface. Mix a contrasting color, and add a blob of glue paint to the wet area. Swirl it around with a toothpick to create a marblelike pattern.

Food colorings are best for basic shades like red, green, yellow, and blue. Watercolors come in a greater variety. Experiment with different combinations on a plain board to find the most attractive one.

When the pattern is complete, set the frame aside in a dry area. It will take two days to dry thoroughly. Spray three coats of acrylic coating for an even sheen. Each coat will take minutes to dry.

Detail Finishing

Cut strips of molding from balsa to fit around the openings in each frame. Glue them in position, overlapping edges to hide unfinished opening in frame. Finish off by gluing velvet ribbon over the molding and around outside edges.

If using an easel, cover it with fabric before attaching to the frame. If no easel is used, cut cardboard to fit the back of the frame, and cover with fabric. In either case, glue the backing to the frame on three sides, leaving room to insert photo in the opening.

The heart frame features a touch of lace all around. Mount this between the frame and the backing. Matching rickrack is glued around both hearts.

Variations

This technique will work on any wood surface as well as on ceramic tile. Consider making trivets.

Making in Quantity

When making Fantasy Frames in quantity, scheduling is important. Two good woodworkers are needed to cut out all frames. This is easily done with a table saw and a jigsaw. You can turn out many frames in a day.

You will need a lot of drying space. If three or four people work together, they can make forty-eight frames in one week. Use the following schedule: cutting frames: one day; applying glue paint: one day; drying: two days; spraying acrylic and finishing details: two days.

Display Ideas

If you have a small wood chest or bureau that is light enough to take to the booth, this will be a nice way to display the frames. A few artifacts that aren't large or distracting add to the effectiveness of the arrangement.

Make a folding screen on which you can hang the frames so they can all be seen at once. The pictures used for display can be your own photographs or cut from magazines. In this way you won't have to remove the photograph each time a frame is sold.

Paper Patchwork Box

Popular patchwork folk patterns are employed for this crafting technique. No sewing is required. Just follow the pattern provided to cover a wooden box with paper pieces cut in the traditional designs of American patchwork quilts.

Every time I use this technique the results are rewarding. In my book *Fabulous Furniture Decorations* I covered a blanket chest with paper patchwork and was delighted to find that when finished, it looked as though it had been covered with fabric patches. The bonus is that it can be protected with varnish and is much easier to do than patchwork.

Materials Needed

5 12-x-12-inch squares of vinyl wallpaper (sample books are often available from wallcovering stores; the papers used for this project are from the miniature collection by Wall-Tex); hinged wooden box (see Source List) 5 inches high by 5½ inches deep and 7 inches wide; Elmer's Glue-All; straightedge; razor blade; tweezers; acrylic paint; pencil; small paintbrush (for painting inside edges); Krylon clear spray varnish.

Directions

Select a variety of wallpaper patterns in light and dark colors. The diamond shapes are based on a traditional star pattern of eight diamonds.

Trace the cutting diagram (see drawing), using a straightedge. Tape the tracing over a layer of five sheets of wall paper. Cut the diamonds out with a straightedge and razor. You will have 60 diamonds. Repeat the process two more times for a total of 180 diamonds, which is more than enough to cover the box.

Draw straight pencil lines from corner to corner

to determine the exact center of the box. Draw a vertical and horizontal line through the center point to line up the first diamond. Complete the center star by gluing each diamond in place with white glue. The design is completed by gluing patches around the center star, making it ever larger until the box is completely covered on all sides except the bottom.

When the box is dry, insert the razor blade into the back of the box where the hinge joins the top and bottom. Pull the razor blade along carefully, cutting the top away from the bottom on all sides.

Cover the inside of the box with one of the wallpaper patterns used on the outside, or make a patchwork design inside, or cover with acrylic paint. If the patchwork design has a strong accent color, paint the inside of the box in that color. Paint the edges with care.

Cut the excess paper away from the hinges. Varnish the entire box with about five coats of clear spray varnish.

Variations

Another popular folk pattern used in patchwork is the box design shown in Diagram B. Cut this

out, and apply in the same way as you did the star. Place the first shape in the center of the top of the box. This is an overall pattern, whereas the star design radiates out from the center star on top.

Making in Quantity

Make a series of small boxes using both these designs. Spray paint the interior of all boxes as well as the inside edges.

You will have a lot of variety in color and patterns without any extra work. Simply use a different set of five sheets of wallpaper for each box,

keeping the directions exactly the same over and over again.

Display Ideas

Make this an Early American display. Collect odds and ends that suggest Americana, and set the stage. Lay out a patchwork quilt, or place rough-hewn wood on a table for holding the boxes. Make pine shelves, and stain in dark walnut. Or sand and stain an old table on which you can arrange the boxes with some dried flowers, a lace doily, or anything else that will complement them.

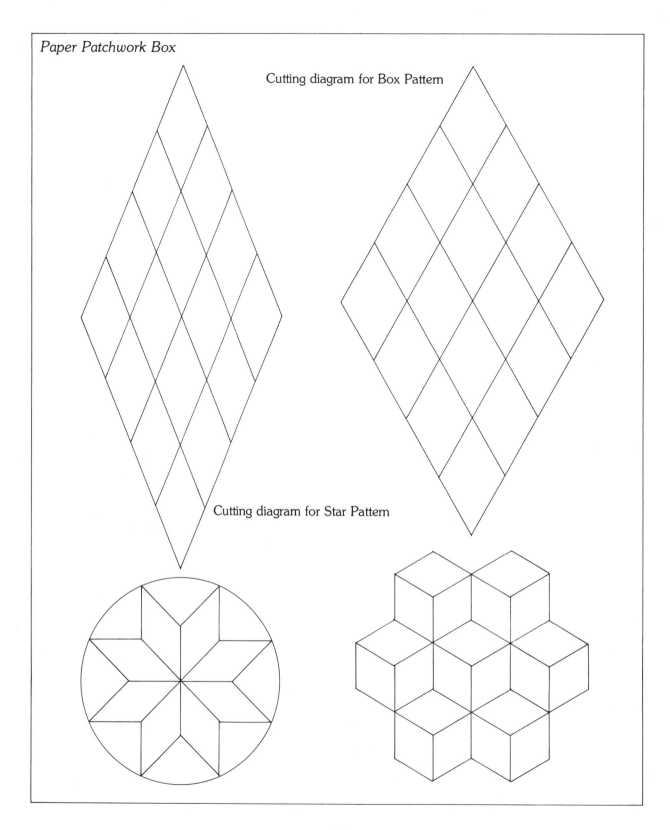

Paper Patchwork Box

Cutting diagram for Box Pattern

Cutting diagram for Star Pattern

Source List of Materials

Almost all of the materials used to make the projects in this book are readily available in local craft and hobby shops or art supply stores. In many cases the materials come from fabric shops, five-and-tens, hardware stores, or your own sewing basket. However, when planning a bazaar there will be many ways in which you can cut costs, and since the goal is to make money you'll want to take advantage of any savings you can realize. Often it is economical to make projects in quantity so that you can buy the materials in bulk. Your local shops may not be in a position to offer a discount that will amount to any real savings. However, because the high overhead of running a store is eliminated in a mail-order business, many people find this a good way to shop for bargains.

The mail-order supply houses listed here have all been contacted in regard to offering a discount to clubs, churches, schools, scouts, and other such community organizations. Most of the prices are below retail to begin with, and these companies offer a further discount for bulk orders over a certain amount of money. In each case the amount necessary to spend is quite reasonable. While there is a small charge for most of the catalogs, this amount is generally applied to the first order.

Some of the catalogs are more extensive than others that show similar items. The prices vary, so leave enough time to compare catalogs before ordering. Study each one and allow four to six weeks to select and order your supplies.

The service from these mail-order companies is quick, efficient, reliable, and courteous. If you have any questions about using the materials, ask and you will almost always receive a reply.

When I was researching companies to include as sources for supplies, I received many long and helpful letters explaining the uses of various products. One, for example, came from Georgia Payne of the Derby Lane Shell Center in Florida. She explained that the shells they carry come from all over the world. They are used for shell mirrors, shell pictures, and jewelry, and the center offers the service of slicing shells for pictures. They also dye them in many colors. Ms. Payne says, "We have a good deal of business with women's clubs needing fund-raising projects. The shells are used by girls' and boys' clubs, and we even have projects for the handicapped. Working with your hands and with things created by nature seems to relax people." Like the other companies, Derby Lane offers a wholesale price for quantity, sometimes as few as one dozen. Do not be afraid to ask for a discount when ordering for a worthy cause.

Art materials

Arthur Brown Inc.
2 West 46th St.
New York, NY 10036

Charrette
31 Olympia Ave.
Woburn, MA 01801
catalog $1.

Baskets

Fran's Basket House
89 W. Main St.
Rockaway, NJ 07866

Bead kits

Enterprise Art
P.O. Box 1041
Largo, FL 33540
catalog $1.

Boxes and wood products

Houston Art and Frame Company
P.O. Box 47164
Houston TX 77027

Nasco Crafts
P.O. Box 15003
Winston-Salem, NC 27103
Wood shapes for jewelry, mobiles,
Christmas ornaments, key chains,
decoupage.

O-P Craft Company
425 Warren St.
Sandusky, OH 44870
catalog $1.

Chicken Coops (for displays)

Cordell Enterprises, Inc.
1622 W. Morse Ave.
Chicago, IL 60626

Crochet and knitting patterns

Anne Lane Originals
P.O. Box 206
North Abington, MA 02351

The Crochet Works
1472 Auburn
Baker, OR 97814
catalog 25¢.

Decals

Meyercord
1010 Mamaroneck Ave.
Mamaroneck, NY 10543

Write to find out where
Meyercord decals are sold in your
area.

Decoupage materials

American Handicrafts
P.O. Box 2911
Fort Worth, TX 76191

O-P Craft Company
425 Warren St.
Sandusky, OH 44870
catalog $1.

Doll and toy patterns

Annie's Attic
Rte 2 Box 212B
Big Sandy, TX 75755
catalog $1.

The Knitting Needle
P.O. Box 31631
Aurora, CO 80041

Platypus
P.O. Box 396
Planetarium Station
New York, NY 10024
catalog $1.

Doll-making supplies

Standard Doll Company
23-83 31st St.
Long Island City, NY 11105
catalog $1.50.

Eggery supplies

Herb Allen's Hole-In-One
3926 Kenosha Ave.
San Diego, CA 92117

Flower-arranging supplies

Dorothy Biddle Service
DBS Building
Hawthorne, NY 10532

Enterprise Art
P.O. Box 1041
Largo, FL 33540
catalog $1.

General crafts

American Handicrafts Company
P.O. Box 2911
Fort Worth, TX 76101

Boycan's Craft Supplies
P.O. Box 897
Sharon, PA 16146

J.L. Hammett Company
Hammett Pl.
Braintree, MA 02184

Jewelry-making materials

Grieger's Incorporated
900 South Arroyo Parkway
Pasadena, CA 91190

Extensive line of jewelry-making supplies. In addition to their catalog, Grieger's, Inc. sends out 4 to 6 sale flyer papers a year. You must ask for them, but there is no charge.

Labels (woven)

Ident-ify Label Corp.
P.O. Box 204
Brooklyn, NY 11214

L. & L. Stitchery
P.O. Box 43821
Atlanta, GA 30336

Needlecraft patterns and kits

Plush Point Patterns
233 East 69th St.
New York, NY 10021

The Stitchery
Dept. 143
Wellesley, MA 02181

Paper bags

Ask for donations from your local supermarkets. Check Yellow Pages for a local paper supplier.

Pine cones

Craft House
P.O. Box 1386
Santa Barbara, CA 93102

Ribbons

Home Sew, Inc.
Bethlehem, PA 18018

Satin patches

Royal Creations
P.O. Box 3201
West End Station
West End, NJ 07740

Seashells

Derby Lane Shell Center
10510 Gandy Blvd.
St. Petersburg FL 33702

Naturecraft
2199 Bancroft Way
Berkeley, CA 94704

Sewing supplies

The Button Treasury
229 West 36th St.
New York, NY 10018

Home-Sew Inc.
Bethlehem, PA 18018

Standard Doll Co.
23-83 31st St.
Long Island City, NY 11105
catalog $1.50.

Silhouettes

Geecraft
Box 391
Blue Earth, MN 56013

Tree Toys
P.O. Box 492
Hinsdale, IL 60521

Stuffed animal and puppet patterns

Fuzzy Friends
by Diane
1126 Ivon Ave.
Endicott, NY 13760
catalog $1.

Ukrainian egg decorating kits

Ukrainian Gift Shop
2422 Central Ave. N.E.
Minneapolis, MN 55418
catalog 25¢.

Velvet

Nucleus Trading Company
P.O. Box 670
Ossining, NY 10562

Yarns and weaving supplies

Mary Lue's
At the Woolen Mill
101 West Broadway
St. Peter, MN 56082

Skillcraft
500 North Calvert St.
Baltimore, MD 21202
catalog $1.

Dear Craftworkers:

All of us who do craftwork learn by doing. The more we work at something the more opportunities we have to discover shortcuts for steps, better ways to handle the material, or clever ways to make the work easier or more enjoyable. When we do the same procedure over and over, we may accidentally find a trick that can make the project turn out better. This can be so simple that we may not even think about it.

Sharing is part of crafting. We share our designs, we share by exposing each other to new projects, and we share by helping with suggested tricks or money-savers that we find useful. Many of you have probably come upon a new method or shortcut that has helped you and would like to pass it on.

As I continue to write craft books and articles and to bring together the work of many craftspeople, I would like to be able to offer your suggestions. If you have anything to share I would very much like to hear from you so that I can include your suggestions in my future writings. In this way we can create a craft idea exchange across the country. Thank you for your help.

Leslie Linsley
c/o Dell Publishing Co., Inc.
1 Dag Hammarskjold Plaza
New York, N.Y. 10017

Index